Spotify Model: Practical Implementation Guide

Marten P. de Jong

Published by Marten P. de Jong, 2023.

While every precaution has been taken in the preparation of this book, the publisher assumes no responsibility for errors or omissions, or for damages resulting from the use of the information contained herein.

SPOTIFY MODEL: PRACTICAL IMPLEMENTATION GUIDE

First edition. July 25, 2023.

ISBN: 979-8223232520

Written by Marten P. de Jong.

Spotify Model

Practical Implementation Guide

Marten P. de Jong

Disclaimer

Foreword

Part 1: Introduction to the Spotify model

    1.1 Necessity of agility and customer orientation

    1.2 What is the Spotify model? An overview

    1.3 Importance of the Spotify model

Part 2: In-depth analysis of the Spotify model

    2.1 Genesis of the Spotify model

    Development and introduction of the model at Spotify

    Important milestones in the history of the model

    Influence of the model on the growth and development phase of Spotify

    2.2 The key elements of the Spotify model - overview

    Detailed explanation of tribes, guilds, squadrons and chapters

    The relationship and interaction between these elements

    The purpose of each element in the overall model

    2.3 Tribes and their role in the Spotify model

    Introduction to the structure and function of logs

The role of tribes in the Spotify model and their interaction with other elements.

Examples of the application of tribes in organizations

Case studies of companies that have successfully deployed tribes

The impact of using tribes on team dynamics and productivity.

2.4 Guilds and their function in the model

Introduction to the structure and function of guilds

The role of guilds in the Spotify model and how they interact with other elements

Examples of the application of guilds in organizations

Case studies of companies that have successfully used guilds

The impact of using guilds on team dynamics and productivity

2.5 Squadron: structure and influence

Introduction to the structure and function of squadrons

The role of squadrons in the Spotify model and how they interact with other elements

Examples of the application of squadrons in organizations

Case studies of companies that have successfully deployed squadrons

The impact of using squadrons on team dynamics and productivity

2.6 Chapters and their meaning

Introduction to the structure and function of chapters

The role of chapters in the Spotify model and their interaction with other elements

Examples of the application of chapters in organizations

Case studies of companies that have successfully used chapters

The impact of using chapters on team dynamics and productivity.

2.7 Success stories and case studies

Detailed case study of an organization that has successfully implemented the Spotify model

Description of the challenges and how they were overcome

Analysis of the impact of the implementation of the Spotify model on the organization

Detailed case study of another organization that has successfully implemented the Spotify model

Description of the challenges and how they were overcome

Analysis of the impact of the implementation of the Spotify model on the organization

Part 3: Implementing the Spotify model in your company

3.1 Assessment of company culture and identification of need for change

How to evaluate the current company culture

Identify the changes needed to implement the Spotify model.

Case studies and examples of adapting company culture to the Spotify model

3.2 Strategies for switching to the Spotify model

Overview of the main steps to implement the Spotify model

Planning and timing for the changeover

Strategies for overcoming challenges during transition

3.3 Communication strategies to accompany the change process

Important points for communication during the changeover

Development of effective communication channels and processes

Case studies and examples of successful communication strategies

3.4 Selection criteria and training procedures for team members

Identify the necessary skills and attributes for team members

Introduction to training procedures and programs for the Spotify model.

Case studies and examples for selection and training of team members

3.5 Setting realistic goals and adjusting expectations over time

How to set realistic goals for moving to the Spotify model

Adjustment of goals and expectations based on progress and feedback

Examples of goal setting and alignment of expectations in organizations that have implemented the Spotify model include

Practical examples and case studies for the implementation of the model

Detailed description of the implementation of the Spotify model in different organizations.

Challenges, successes and lessons learned from these examples

Guidance on how to apply these insights in your own business

SPOTIFY MODEL: PRACTICAL IMPLEMENTATION GUIDE

Part 4: Measure success and make adjustments

4.1 Selection and definition of metrics

Overview of possible metrics for measuring the success of the Spotify model

How to define metrics that best reflect the success of the model

Case studies and examples of the successful application of metrics

4.2 Monitoring progress

Methods and tools for monitoring the progress of the transition to the Spotify model

How to create and interpret progress reports

Case studies and examples of effective monitoring of progress

4.3 Evaluation of the results

Evaluating the Implementation of the Spotify Model: A Practice Guide

Make changes and adjust plans based on evaluation results

Case studies and examples for the evaluation of results and resulting changes

4.4 Strategy adjustments based on performance

Adjustment of the implementation strategy based on performance data

Involving employees in the process of strategy adaptation

Case studies and examples of strategy adaptations in organizations that have implemented the Spotify model

4.5 Iterative improvements

Introduction to the concept of iterative improvement in the context of the Spotify model.

How to collect and use feedback to make iterative improvements

Case studies and examples of iterative improvements in organizations that have implemented the Spotify model.

Part 5: Further development of the Spotify model

5.1 Further improvements in cooperation

Techniques and strategies to further improve collaboration within the Spotify model.

How to use feedback and evaluation systems to improve collaboration

Case studies and examples of successful collaboration improvements

5.2 Promoting agility in the organization

Methods for promoting agility in teams and the entire organization

Application of agile principles to organizational structure and processes

Case studies and examples of successfully improved agility

5.3 Optimization of customer orientation

Strategies for improving customer focus using the Spotify model.

Integration of customer feedback and adaptation of processes to improve customer orientation

Case studies and examples of successfully improved customer orientation

5.4 Adaptations and modifications of the model

Overview of possible adjustments to the Spotify model to improve performance.

How to make changes based on the specific needs and challenges of the business

Case studies and examples of successful modifications to the Spotify model.

5.5 Looking to the future: further developments and trends

Predictions and expectations for the future of the Spotify model

MARTEN P. DE JONG

Trends and innovations in agile organizational development

Case studies and examples of innovative applications and advancements of the Spotify model.

Disclaimer

This book is intended for informational purposes only. While every effort has been made to ensure that the information and advice provided in this book is accurate and up-to-date, the author and publisher assume no responsibility or liability for any errors, omissions, inaccuracies, or other discrepancies.

The case studies and examples included in this book are based on real experiences and circumstances, but all company and organization names have been largely anonymized to meet confidentiality and privacy requirements.

Although this book contains best practices and advice for applying the Spotify model to improve customer focus, it is the reader's responsibility to assess the suitability and applicability of this information to their specific circumstances. The author and publisher assume no liability for any damages or losses that may result directly or indirectly from the implementation of the information contained in this book.

The reader is encouraged to seek professional advice before making any significant changes to their organization or business. It is important to understand that although the Spotify model offers many benefits, it is not suitable for every organization and its implementation must be carefully planned and managed.

The opinions and views expressed in this book are those of the author and do not necessarily reflect the opinions and views of the publisher or its contributors.

Foreword

It is with great pleasure that I present this book, which is a result of many years of intensive research and practical experience in the world of agile organizational structures.

When I first started exploring the topic of the Spotify model, I, like many others, was intrigued by the potential impact of this revolutionary approach. Many books have described and analyzed the implementation of the Spotify model in detail. They offer deep insight into Spotify's success story. However, what I found lacking in many of these books was practical guidance on how to apply this success story to other contexts.

I was particularly concerned not to design this book as a purely informational work that only presents the implementation at Spotify, but rather to create a practical guide that provides organizations and companies with the necessary information and tools to decide whether approaches from the Spotify model make sense for them and how they can implement them in a positive case.

To achieve this goal, I have included a variety of checklists, examples, and detailed instructions in the book. These are designed to help you identify, select, and implement the aspects of the Spotify model that are relevant to your organization. It's about adapting the principles and practices of the Spotify model to your organization's specific needs and challenges, while achieving the greatest possible value.

I hope you find this book not only informative, but also inspiring, and that it helps you identify and seize new opportunities for your organization. It is my deep belief that the Spotify model, when applied correctly, can help make organizations more nimble, effective, and customer-centric.

With this in mind, I invite you to dive into the exciting world of the Spotify model. May this book be your faithful companion on this journey.

Part 1: Introduction to the Spotify model

1.1 Necessity of agility and customer orientation

The Modern Business World and the Role of Agility

In today's rapidly changing business world, it is essential to be able to respond to change. The ability of an organization to flexibly adapt to market changes is referred to as agility. Agility is a mindset that incorporates both proactivity and reactivity, enabling organizations to respond to change without losing focus on their long-term goals.

Companies that are agile can respond quickly and effectively to change, seize new opportunities and avoid risks. They strive to improve internal processes, adapt ways of working, and find creative solutions to problems. In an agile organization, the focus is on learning, with failures seen as learning opportunities rather than obstacles.

Customer orientation as a competitive advantage

In today's business world, it is no longer enough to simply offer a good product or service. To survive in an increasingly competitive market, companies must focus on their customers and see them as the main drivers of their business. This approach is known as customer orientation.

Customer-centric companies focus on meeting the needs and expectations of their customers. They collect and analyze customer data to understand behavioral patterns, deliver personalized experiences, and ultimately increase customer satisfaction and loyalty. A strong customer focus can lead to higher customer loyalty, improved reputation and ultimately increased business success.

Case studies in which agility and customer focus have led to success

Amazon is an excellent example of a company that has made agility and customer focus the cornerstone of its business model. Despite its size, Amazon has cultivated a culture of agility that has enabled it to respond quickly to change and develop innovative products and services. At the same time, Amazon is known for putting its customers first. This customer-centric approach has given Amazon a significant competitive advantage and helped it become a leader in the global retail landscape.

Another notable example is Spotify, the music streaming company that developed the model we will explore in this book. By implementing an agile model based on teamwork, autonomy, and continuous improvement, Spotify has been able to consolidate and expand its market position. At the same time, Spotify's consistent customer focus has created an intuitive and personalized listening experience that sets it apart from the competition.

In summary, agility and customer focus are crucial factors for success in the modern business world. They enable companies to respond quickly to change, develop innovative solutions, and focus on their customers. Companies that internalize and implement these principles are well positioned to succeed in today's fast-paced and customer-centric business environment.

1.2 What is the Spotify model? An overview

Origins and developers of the Spotify model

The Spotify model is a way of organizing work that was originally developed by the Swedish music streaming service Spotify. The creators of Spotify, Henrik Kniberg and Anders Ivarsson, created a model that combines agility and efficiency to create an optimal work environment. The structure of this model allows teams to act flexibly and autonomously while working towards common business goals.

Brief description of the main components of the model

The Spotify model is based on four main components called Squads, Tribes, Chapters and Guilds.

A squad is the basic work team in the Spotify model. It is a small, cross-functional group dedicated to a specific project or product area. Each squad has a high level of autonomy and is responsible for developing its own working methods and achieving its goals.

Tribes consist of multiple squads working on related projects or product areas. A tribe leader oversees the work of the squads, provides support, and facilitates communication between teams.

Chapters are discipline-specific groups within a Squad or Tribe. Members of a chapter share a similar specialty or skill and work together to share knowledge and develop best practices.

Finally, there are the Guilds, informal networks that transcend the boundaries of Squads and Tribes and bring together people with similar interests or areas of expertise to share knowledge and ideas.

Application areas of the Spotify model

The Spotify model can be applied in many different types of organizations and in different industries. It is particularly effective in companies that value innovation and rapid growth, as it promotes the flexibility and autonomy necessary to achieve these goals.

In addition, the Spotify model is an attractive option for organizations seeking to transform towards agility. It provides a framework that can help organizations develop and implement agile working practices. It is important to note that the Spotify model is not a rigid set of rules, but rather a flexible framework that can be adapted depending on the specific needs and challenges of an organization.

In short, the Spotify model is an innovative framework that enables organizations to drive agility, improve collaboration, and respond quickly to market changes.

1.3 Importance of the Spotify model

Why the Spotify model is relevant today

The Spotify model has proven particularly relevant in the rapidly changing business world, where companies are looking for ways to be agile, flexible and innovative. At a time when traditional organizational structures are often seen as too rigid and inefficient, the Spotify model offers a refreshing alternative. It enables companies to modernize the way they work and increase efficiency while creating an environment that fosters creativity and innovation.

Impact of the Spotify model on team structure and productivity

The Spotify model has a significant impact on the way teams are structured and how they collaborate. By creating small, autonomous squads, the model enables faster decision-making and greater flexibility. Because each squad is responsible for achieving its own goals, ownership is fostered and a strong sense of team identity is created.

In addition, the Spotify model supports continuous improvement and learning by encouraging knowledge sharing and collaboration across squads. This type of environment can lead to increased productivity and employee satisfaction.

Comparison of the Spotify model with traditional work models

Compared to traditional work models, which are often based on hierarchical and rigid structures, the Spotify model offers a flatter and more flexible organizational structure. While traditional models typically have clear chains of command and defined roles, the Spotify model emphasizes autonomy, ownership, and collaboration.

In the Spotify model, leadership roles still exist, but they serve as support and mentors rather than issuing orders. This approach can help increase job satisfaction and foster a sense of ownership and engagement among employees.

Overall, the Spotify model can be seen as a progressive response to the challenges of the modern working world. It offers a flexible and agile alternative to traditional work models that can boost employee creativity, productivity and satisfaction.

Part 2: In-depth analysis of the Spotify model

2.1 Genesis of the Spotify model

The genesis of the Spotify model is closely linked to the development of the music streaming company Spotify itself. Founded in Sweden in 2006, Spotify fundamentally changed the music industry by launching a streaming service that gave users access to millions of songs on demand. But the company's innovative approach wasn't limited to its product. Spotify also set new standards in terms of work organization.

As the company grew, so did the complexity of projects and the need for an efficient and effective organizational structure. Management was looking for ways to increase agility and productivity while maintaining the company's culture of innovation and creativity.

In this situation, Spotify executives Henrik Kniberg and Anders Ivarsson created the Spotify model. Their vision was to create an organizational structure that leveraged the advantages of small teams - namely their agility, autonomy and creativity - while scaling them across a larger organization. Their approach was heavily inspired by agile methods, but they adapted it to Spotify's specific needs and challenges.

The result was an innovative organizational structure based on four main components: Squads, Tribes, Chapters and Guilds. Each element plays a critical role in the Spotify model and helps achieve the goals of agility, autonomy and effectiveness.

The Spotify model quickly became popular and many other companies, especially in the tech sector, began incorporating elements of it into their own organizational structures. Although the model is not intended to be a universal solution for all organizations, it has proven to be a valuable tool for improving the organization of work in fast-paced and innovative environments.

The emergence of the Spotify model shows how a company can create innovative solutions by adapting proven methods to its specific needs and challenges. It is an example of how organizational structure itself can become a factor in innovation and success.

Development and introduction of the model at Spotify

The development and implementation of the Spotify model at Spotify itself was a process characterized by experimentation and constant adaptation. The model did not emerge from a set plan, but was born out of the company's continuous pursuit of improvement and efficiency.

The first steps in implementing the model began with the formation of smaller, cross-functional teams called "squads." These squads were formed with the goal of achieving a high degree of autonomy. Each squad was responsible for a specific aspect of the product and had the freedom to make decisions and determine its own way of working.

However, the company quickly realized that collaboration and communication between squads needed to be improved to ensure coherent product development. This need gave rise to the concepts of "Tribes" and "Guilds." Tribes are groups of squads working on related product areas, while Guilds represent communities of individuals with similar expertise or interests. These structures enabled improved sharing of knowledge and ideas across squad boundaries.

Eventually, the concept of "chapters" emerged in response to the need to provide some type of line management and professional development within the flat organizational structure. A chapter is a group of people within a tribe who have a similar role or expertise and are led by a chapter lead.

The development and implementation of the Spotify model was thus an evolutionary process based on Spotify's specific needs and challenges. It was an approach that required constant adaptation and improvement, always keeping in mind the main goal: to create an agile and efficient organizational structure that fosters creativity and innovation.

Spotify's experience shows that implementing such a model is not a linear or simple process. It requires experimentation, open communication, and a willingness to make mistakes and learn from them. But the result can be an organizational structure that significantly improves teamwork, productivity, and employee satisfaction.

Important milestones in the history of the model

In the development history of the Spotify model, some significant milestones can be identified that have shaped the model and fostered its diffusion and acceptance in the tech community.

2008: Spotify founded - This was the year Spotify was founded by Daniel Ek and Martin Lorentzon in Sweden. From the beginning, they focused on a culture of innovation and continuous improvement, which ultimately led to the development of the Spotify model.

2012: First mention of the Spotify model - In 2012, the first discussions and presentations publicly describing the Spotify model began. These early descriptions primarily emphasized the importance of team autonomy and ownership.

2014: Spotify Model Video Release - One of the most significant milestones in the history of the Spotify model was the company's release of two videos that explained the model and its components in detail. These videos were instrumental in raising awareness of the Spotify model in the tech community and increasing its influence and adoption.

2015-2020: Dissemination and application of the model - In the following years, the Spotify model was adopted in many tech companies and organizations around the world. During this time, the model was further refined and adapted, and much discussion and research emerged about its effectiveness and applicability.

2021 and beyond: further development and criticism - More recently, there have been both further developments and criticisms of the Spotify model. Some critics complain that the model is too tailored to Spotify's specific needs and therefore not universally applicable. Despite these criticisms, however, the Spotify model remains a popular and influential approach in the world of agile development.

These milestones illustrate how the Spotify model has grown from an internal working method to a model that is respected worldwide and applied in different contexts. However, it remains a model in need of constant adaptation and improvement and should never be considered a finished product.

Influence of the model on the growth and development phase of Spotify

The impact of the Spotify model on Spotify's growth and development phase cannot be overlooked. It has played a significant role in how the company has evolved and has had a lasting impact on Spotify's cultural identity.

Accelerating product innovation: Through autonomous, interdisciplinary teams, also known as "squads," Spotify was able to dramatically reduce the time spent on product development. These squads were able to work autonomously and independently of each other and drive innovation quickly. This enabled Spotify to bring new features to market faster than its competitors, thereby strengthening its market position.

Fostering a learning organization: The Spotify model emphasizes the concept of continuous learning and improvement. By implementing feedback loops and regular retrospective meetings in squads, Spotify was able to create an environment where continuous learning and improvement became the norm. This has helped increase the company's adaptability and foster employee development.

Increase employee satisfaction: The autonomy and sense of ownership that the Spotify model gives to squads has contributed to employee satisfaction and motivation. By allowing each squad to make its own decisions and have direct influence on the final product, Spotify has been able to achieve greater retention and engagement among its employees.

Adaptability to change: The Spotify model allowed the company to remain flexible and adaptable even as it grew rapidly. The autonomous and decentralized structure of the squads enabled Spotify to quickly adapt to change and respond to market changes.

Overall, the Spotify model has played a central role in shaping Spotify's corporate culture and strategy. It has fostered Spotify's growth and development and helped the company establish itself as a leader in the music streaming industry.

2.2 The key elements of the Spotify model - overview

The Spotify model consists of several unique elements that interact and collaborate to create a flexible and agile work environment. These elements are specifically designed to foster collaboration, facilitate learning, and cultivate an innovative company culture. Let's take a closer look at these key elements:

1. Squads: In Spotify, Squads are the basic working units consisting of a small group of people with different skills. Each squad has a specific goal or mission that it pursues independently. The autonomy of these squads encourages entrepreneurship and creativity within the company.

2. tribes: multiple squads working on similar or related topics are grouped into larger groups called tribes. Tribes enable information sharing and collaboration between squads, foster community, and support consistency across projects.

3. chapters: within tribes, individuals with similar expertise or roles organize themselves into so-called chapters. These groups serve to share best practices, develop skills, and cultivate a supportive community within the specific discipline.

4. guilds: Unlike chapters, which are often organized within a tribe, guilds are enterprise-wide communities of interest that span across different tribes and squads. They serve to share knowledge and best practices across the enterprise.

5. Agile Coach: Each Tribe has one or more Agile Coaches who help implement and promote Agile practices and support continuous improvement within the teams.

Together, these key elements form the backbone of the Spotify model. They promote autonomy and ownership, enhance collaboration and information sharing, and support a culture of continuous learning and improvement.

Detailed explanation of tribes, guilds, squadrons and chapters

The organizational units of the Spotify model, called "Squads," "Tribes," "Chapters," and "Guilds," each have specific roles and responsibilities. Here is a more detailed explanation of these elements.

Squadrons (Squads): A squad is the smallest unit in the Spotify model and is essentially equivalent to a Scrum team. A squad typically consists of 6 to 12 people with different expertise needed to accomplish the given tasks. This can include software developers, testers, product managers, and UX designers. Each squad is responsible for a specific aspect of the product and works autonomously on it. The autonomy enables the squad to make decisions and thus react quickly and flexibly to changes.

Tribes (Tribes): A Tribe is a collection of Squads working in a specific business area or on a product area. A Tribe is usually led by a Tribe Leader and typically includes up to 150 people. The purpose of the Tribe is to facilitate collaboration and communication between Squads and to ensure that all Squads are working in the same direction.

Chapter (Chapters): A chapter is a type of vertical structure within the Spotify model that focuses on a specific discipline such as testing, data analysis, or user interface design. People working in different squads can belong to the same chapter if they have similar skills or areas of expertise. A chapter is led by a chapter leader, who also acts as a line manager and is responsible for the professional development of chapter members.

Guilds (Guilds): A guild is an informal organizational unit that allows individuals from across the organization to gather around a common interest or area of expertise. Guilds are organic in nature and can be created by anyone in the organization. They serve as a platform for knowledge sharing and collaborative problem solving, and are often used to spread best practices and new ideas throughout the organization.

These organizational structures work together to promote autonomy and collaboration, share knowledge, and foster innovation across the enterprise. The uniqueness of each element and their interactions make the Spotify model a powerful tool for agile working practices.

The relationship and interaction between these elements

The beauty of the Spotify model lies in the way these different entities - squadrons, tribes, chapters, and guilds - interact and collaborate with each other. This collaboration allows for a balance between autonomy and alignment that is essential to both individual creativity and shared business goals.

Interaction between squadrons and tribes: Squadrons are independent teams that share a common goal and organize their work autonomously. However, they are not in isolation. Multiple squadrons working on similar or related product areas are grouped into a tribe. Tribes serve to maintain a broader perspective and ensure that squadrons are working toward a common goal while creating an environment that fosters the exchange of ideas and best practices.

Interaction between squadrons and chapters: Members of a squadron often also belong to a chapter. A chapter is a group of individuals who have similar expertise or skills and occupy the same role in different squadrons. By belonging to a chapter, individuals can share expertise, improve skills, and discuss career development plans with the chapter leader (who also acts as their line manager).

Interaction between squadrons, chapters, and guilds: While chapters are formal structures with a specific reporting path, guilds are informal, cross-functional groups grouped around a common interest or area of expertise. Anyone with an interest in the guild's topic can join, regardless of which squadron or chapter they belong to. Guilds provide a platform where employees can share knowledge, spread best practices, and solve common problems.

These complementary entities promote autonomy by allowing squadrons to operate independently while ensuring extensive collaboration and communication through tribes, chapters, and guilds. This creates a balance between autonomy and collaboration that is critical to agility and innovation in the Spotify model.

The purpose of each element in the overall model

In the Spotify model, each element - squadrons, tribes, chapters, and guilds - has a specific role to fulfill and helps make the entire system efficient, productive, and innovative.

Purpose of Squadrons: Squadrons are the building blocks of the Spotify model. They are cross-functional teams that work on a specific product area or feature. They are autonomous and decide how to get their work done, which encourages flexibility and creativity. Their main task is to develop and improve the products that Spotify's customers use.

Purpose of Tribes: Tribes serve to bring together squadrons working on similar or related product areas. They provide a sense of belonging, encourage communication and sharing of best practices, and ensure that all squadrons are working in the same direction. They ensure that the company as a whole is working toward a common goal.

Purpose of Chapters: Chapters are groups of individuals who have similar expertise or skills and occupy the same role in different squadrons. They are used to share expertise, improve skills, and discuss career development plans. Chapters promote professional excellence and personal development of their members.

Purpose of Guilds: Guilds are informal, cross-functional groups that cluster around a common interest or area of expertise. They provide a platform for knowledge sharing, dissemination of best practices, and problem solving. They foster learning, innovation, and collaboration across the organization.

Taken together, these four elements ensure that the Spotify model fosters individual autonomy and creativity as well as organizational alignment and collaboration, resulting in a dynamic, agile, and customer-centric work environment.

2.3 Tribes and their role in the Spotify model

Tribes are an essential part of the Spotify model, a framework that helps companies operate in an agile and customer-centric way. In this section, we will take a closer look at tribes, their tasks, their role, and how they contribute to the performance and efficiency of the overall model.

A tribe in the Spotify model is basically a collection of squadrons working on related or similar product or project areas. A tribe could be considered a sort of "mini-company" within the company proper, with its own squadrons (teams) working independently of each other, but still towards common goals. Tribes can vary in size, but should always be kept at a level that allows for effective communication and collaboration. It is important to emphasize that tribes should not be viewed as hierarchical entities, but rather as functional and collaborative groups.

The role of tribes in this model is multifaceted. One of the main benefits is that they enable effective collaboration and communication between squadrons. As squadrons in a tribe work on similar or related projects, they can share best practices, learning experiences, and resources with each other, which increases efficiency and productivity.

In addition, tribes create a strong sense of community and belonging among their members. They foster a culture of mutual support and sharing that not only improves work results, but also increases employee engagement and satisfaction.

Another important aspect of tribes in the Spotify model is alignment. By setting clear, common goals for all of their squadrons, they ensure that all teams are headed in the same direction and align their efforts to achieve those goals. This ensures that the company as a whole is working toward its strategic goals and helps avoid deviation and misalignment.

However, the role of tribes does not end with coordinating and supporting squadrons. They also play a critical role in fostering innovation and learning. They encourage squadrons to explore and try out new ideas and provide a platform for sharing knowledge and experiences. They foster an environment where continuous learning and improvement becomes the norm.

In summary, tribes play a critical role in the Spotify model. They bring squadrons together, foster collaboration and sharing, provide alignment, and promote innovation and learning. Through their role, they are instrumental in enabling the Spotify model to be agile, efficient, and customer-centric. They are the glue that holds the model together and the engine that drives it.

Introduction to the structure and function of logs

The structure and function of tribes are essential aspects of the Spotify model. They influence both the way work is organized and performed, and the culture and dynamics within the company.

A tribe in the Spotify model is a larger organizational unit that consists of multiple squadrons. A squadron is a small, cross-functional team focused on a specific product or aspect of a product. Multiple squadrons working on related or complementary projects form a tribe. It is important to note that despite their size, tribes should remain agile. This means that they can adapt and respond quickly to change.

The structure of a tribe is designed to promote autonomy and personal responsibility. Each squadron within the tribe has control over its working methods, decision-making processes, and priorities. This allows for faster decision making and reduces the bureaucracy often found in traditional organizational structures.

The function of tribes goes beyond mere organizational structure. They also serve as a catalyst for collaboration and learning. Within a tribe, squadrons share knowledge, ideas, and best practices. This fosters a culture of continuous learning and improvement.

Additionally, tribes foster a strong community and supportive culture. They provide a kind of "home" for squadrons and create an environment where employees feel safe to take risks and innovate.

In summary, tribes in the Spotify model are not only an organizational entity, but also a driving force for agility, collaboration, and innovation. Through their structure and function, they enable squadrons to operate effectively and efficiently while fostering a culture based on continuous learning, adaptability, and support. They are an essential building block of the Spotify model and a key contributor to its performance and success.

The role of tribes in the Spotify model and their interaction with other elements.

Tribes occupy a central role in the landscape of the Spotify model. As groupings of related squadrons, they provide structure and community, but their function extends far beyond these basic aspects.

Tribes act as incubators for innovation and creativity. Because they emphasize autonomy and ownership, they encourage their squadrons to develop new ideas and experiment. They foster the freedom to try different approaches, learning what works and what doesn't. This stimulating environment can lead to remarkable innovations.

In terms of interaction with other elements of the Spotify model, tribes also play an important role. They are the bridge between squadrons and the other organizational levels - guilds and chapters.

Guilds are interdisciplinary, thematic groups that pool expertise in specific areas, such as data management or user experience. An employee can be a member of multiple guilds, broadening their horizons and deepening their knowledge in different areas. This is where tribes can play a mediating role by facilitating the sharing of knowledge and best practices between squadrons and guilds.

Chapters, on the other hand, are discipline-specific groups formed within a tribe and led by a chapter leader. Chapters serve as a platform for professional development and knowledge sharing among members of a discipline. Within a tribe, they provide for professional exchange and continuous improvement of skills.

The interaction between tribes, guilds and chapters is a key feature of the Spotify model. These elements are not isolated from each other, but interact in a dynamic and symbiotic way. They complement and support each other, which contributes to the overall effectiveness and adaptability of the model.

In summary, tribes in the Spotify model are not just organizational entities. Rather, they are engines for innovation, bridge builders for collaboration, and catalysts for continuous learning and improvement. Through their interactions with squadrons, guilds, and chapters, they contribute significantly to the dynamics and performance of the Spotify model.

Examples of the application of tribes in organizations

The use of tribes in the organizational structure is a fundamental feature of the Spotify model, but it can be applied in other companies as well. Here are some examples of how different organizations have integrated tribes into their structure.

One of the most prominent examples is, of course, Spotify itself. The organization is divided into different tribes, each containing a group of squadrons. Each tribe is focused on a specific product or service, such as the mobile app, desktop client, or data infrastructure. This organizational division allows each tribe to focus on its specific tasks while having the ability to collaborate and share knowledge with other tribes.

Another example is ABC, one of the largest banks in the world. ABC has overhauled its traditional, hierarchical structure and taken the Spotify model as the basis for its organizational structure. The bank has divided its IT department into "tribes," each covering a specific aspect of IT operations, such as infrastructure, data management or mobile applications. This reorganization has led to more autonomy and ownership and paved the way for a culture of continuous learning and improvement.

Another example is the gaming industry, where companies like Riot Games and Electronic Arts have introduced similar tribal structures. In these companies, teams working on different games or game components are grouped into "tribes." This structure encourages collaboration and knowledge sharing between teams and helps create a vibrant and creative company culture.

These examples illustrate that the use of tribes in organizational structure goes far beyond Spotify. They can be an effective way to foster collaboration, autonomy and innovation, regardless of the company's industry or field of activity.

Case studies of companies that have successfully deployed tribes

There are numerous examples of companies that have successfully adopted the idea of tribes from the Spotify model. Let's look at two impressive case studies: Bank ABC and global technology company GEx.

ABC: An agile bank

ABC, one of the largest banks in the Netherlands, decided to make a radical change in its way of working in 2015. It adapted the Spotify model and organized its IT staff into tribes. Each tribe was focused on a specific business area, such as payments, customer interaction or risk management.

This restructuring enabled ABC to achieve its goals faster and more efficiently. The new teams, organized into tribes and squadrons, were able to work autonomously, resulting in accelerated decision-making and improved product development. In addition, the tribal structure fostered a culture of continuous learning and improvement as it encouraged employees to learn new skills and share existing knowledge.

GEx: Transformation to Agility

GEx, a global leader in information and communications technology, also implemented the Spotify model in parts of its organization. The company formed "tribes" around specific technology domains and introduced "squadrons" and "guilds" in line with the principles of agility and continuous improvement.

Adopting the Spotify model led to significant improvements at GEx. Projects ran more smoothly, and product delivery times were dramatically reduced. In addition, the company reported improved job satisfaction and higher employee engagement.

These two case studies impressively demonstrate how the tribal structure of the Spotify model can be successfully applied in different business contexts. It shows that this type of organization is not only suitable for technology companies or start-ups, but can also be used effectively in more traditional industries, such as banking. It emphasizes the universality and adaptability of the model and its value as a tool to promote agility and continuous improvement.

The impact of using tribes on team dynamics and productivity.

Implementing the tribal concept in organizations can have profound effects on team dynamics and productivity. Through the specific structure and function of tribes, organizations can improve the flow of communication, strengthen accountability, and increase productivity.

Increase team cohesion

Teams organized in tribes often exhibit increased cohesion. Because members of a tribe often work closely together and share similar goals, there is a sense of belonging and common purpose. This can facilitate collaboration and conflict resolution within the team, improving team dynamics.

Communication improvement

The structure of the tribes promotes open and transparent communication. Because members of a tribe are in close contact with each other and collaborate frequently, information can flow more easily and quickly. This can help avoid misunderstandings and speed up decision-making.

Increasing responsibility

In a tribe, members often take greater responsibility for their work. Because teams operate autonomously and members are engaged, they are more likely to feel responsible for the results of their work. This can increase motivation and productivity.

Increase productivity

The structure of the tribes can also help to increase productivity. Because the teams can act autonomously and make decisions quickly, they can work more efficiently. In addition, the open and transparent communication within the tribes promotes problem solving and innovation.

In conclusion, the use of tribes in organizations can significantly impact team dynamics and productivity. It promotes greater collaboration, improves communication, increases accountability, and boosts productivity. It is therefore not surprising that more and more companies are adapting this model to improve their performance.

2.4 Guilds and their function in the model

In the context of the Spotify model, a guild refers to a group of people within an organization who share a common interest or expertise. Unlike tribes and squadrons, which tend to focus on specific projects or product areas, guilds are spread throughout the organization and connect people who work on different projects but have similar skills or knowledge.

A guild is usually an informal and loosely organized group. Membership and participation in a guild is usually voluntary and open to everyone in the organization, regardless of their role or project. The primary role of a guild is to provide a forum for the exchange of ideas and best practices, as well as to promote continuing education and learning within its domain of expertise.

Guilds function

Guilds play a central role in the Spotify model. They provide an effective means of fostering knowledge sharing, collaboration, and continuous improvement across projects and teams. Guilds serve to share expertise and best practices, generate new ideas, and foster innovation. They provide a platform where individuals can learn, improve their skills, and benefit from each other.

Guilds are often responsible for creating and maintaining common standards and practices within their domain of expertise. They can also serve as a platform for coordinating initiatives and projects related to their specific domain of expertise. For example, a guild of software developers might develop and enforce standards for coding and software testing practices, while a guild of UX designers might develop guidelines for user interface design.

In addition, guilds can help strengthen the sense of belonging and community within the organization. They can encourage employees to maintain relationships beyond their daily work and to network within the organization.

Summary

Overall, guilds in the Spotify model are an important mechanism for fostering knowledge sharing, learning, and collaboration. By providing an open forum for the exchange of ideas and best practices, they support continuous improvement and innovation. At the same time, they help foster a stronger sense of community and broader networking within the organization.

Introduction to the structure and function of guilds

The word "guild" inevitably conjures up images of medieval guilds and brotherhoods. In the Spotify model, however, a guild is something completely different. A guild is an organic and sprawling community of individuals who share a particular expertise or area of interest. They are spread across the organization, cross team and department boundaries, and are not tied to specific projects or product areas.

The structure of a guild in the Spotify model is usually loose and informal. There are usually no set membership requirements or formal roles within a guild. Anyone in the organization who has an interest in the guild's area of expertise can become a member and participate. Membership in a guild is voluntary and based on a shared interest and passion for a particular area of expertise.

The function of a guild is primarily to serve as a forum for sharing knowledge and experiences. Guilds allow employees to connect across projects and teams, exchange ideas, learn from each other, and share best practices. They can also serve as a platform to create and maintain common standards and practices within their area of expertise.

In addition to these functional roles, guilds also play a social role within the organization. They foster a sense of community and collaboration by enabling employees to build relationships and networks beyond their immediate teams. In this sense, guilds also foster collaboration and communication across the organization.

Overall, guilds in the Spotify model function as vibrant and dynamic communities of learning and sharing. They provide the foundation for a culture of continuous improvement and innovation, and help foster a stronger sense of community and collaboration within the organization.

The role of guilds in the Spotify model and how they interact with other elements

Guilds play a critical role in the Spotify model by providing a platform for professional exchange and continuous learning opportunities. Their primary role is to promote the sharing of knowledge and best practices within their domain of expertise. They serve as platforms for peer-to-peer learning, enabling members to improve their skills, acquire new knowledge, and learn from the experiences of their peers.

Guilds interact with other elements of the Spotify model in various ways, particularly squadrons, tribes, and chapters. They enable organizational connection across teams and foster collaboration across different areas and domains. Here are some examples of how guilds interact with other elements:

- With squadrons: Members of a squadron who are interested in the same area of expertise can join the same guild to keep up to date, expand their knowledge, and learn from others. In this context, guilds can help deepen expertise within a squadron and improve team effectiveness.

- With tribes: Guilds cross tribal boundaries and allow members to network with colleagues across the organization. In this way, they can help break down silos, foster collaboration, and strengthen the sense of community within the organization.

- With chapters: Guilds and chapters can often cover similar areas of expertise. While chapters aim to deepen expertise in specific roles within a tribe, guilds enable the sharing of expertise across different roles and teams. They can be seen as complementary to chapters to provide a broader perspective and knowledge sharing.

Overall, guilds are an integral part of the Spotify model. They play a critical role in fostering knowledge sharing, collaboration, and continuous learning, helping to create a dynamic and learning-oriented culture.

Examples of the application of guilds in organizations

The use of guilds in organizations can take many forms, depending on the specific needs and goals of the organization. Here are some examples of the ways guilds can be used in different contexts:

In software companies: In a typical software company, guilds might be organized around specific technologies or practices. For example, there might be a Java Guild, a Data Science Guild, or an Agile Guild. Members of these guilds meet regularly to share their expertise, discuss common challenges, and exchange best practices. In this way, guilds contribute to the continuous improvement of technical skills and agile practices in the company.

In consulting firms: In a consulting firm, guilds could be used to promote specific industry expertise. For example, there could be a healthcare guild, a financial services guild, or a retail guild. These guilds would focus on deepening understanding of specific industry dynamics, customer needs, and regulatory requirements. They could hold regular meetings to discuss industry-related news, present case studies, and share insights from successful projects.

In nonprofit organizations: In a nonprofit organization, guilds could be used to support specific mission areas. For example, there could be a fundraising guild, a marketing guild, or a volunteer management guild. Members of these guilds could focus on improving their knowledge and skills in these specific areas, developing effective strategies, and contributing innovative ideas.

These examples illustrate that the application of guilds in organizations can be diverse and flexible. They can be adapted to the specific needs and goals of each organization and play an important role in promoting professional excellence and continuous improvement.

Case studies of companies that have successfully used guilds

It is enlightening to examine how different organizations have implemented and used guilds. Let's go through some real-world examples to illustrate what these applications might look like in practice.

Case study 1: BST

BST has employed the use of guilds to foster a continuous learning culture. They have created a number of guilds centered around specific technology areas such as Java, cloud platforms, or artificial intelligence. These guilds regularly host what they call "learning sessions" where members can share their knowledge and have discussions. As a result, BST has reported that this initiative has contributed to improved collaboration, faster knowledge transfer and increased employee engagement.

Case study 2: ABC Bank

ABC Bank has also implemented guilds, but with a slightly different focus. Instead of focusing on specific technologies, they have organized guilds around specific specialist functions. For example, there are guilds for Data Science, Project Management, and User Experience Design. These guilds provide a platform for sharing best practices, organizing training and workshops, and conducting joint projects. According to ABC, these guilds have helped create a stronger professional community within the bank and accelerate knowledge transfer.

Case study 3: Spotify

Of course, no discussion of guilds would be complete without mentioning Spotify, the company that popularized the concept. At Spotify, guilds are interdisciplinary groups that cluster around a common interest or area of expertise. They can be as specific as "web development" or as broad as "leadership." Guilds at Spotify are responsible for providing training, creating best practices, and fostering innovation. Spotify has reported that this structure has led to improved collaboration, stronger learning, and increased innovation.

These case studies show that guilds can be implemented in organizations in a variety of ways and that they can bring numerous benefits. They are flexible structures that can be used to promote professional excellence, accelerate learning and innovation, and improve employee retention.

The impact of using guilds on team dynamics and productivity

Implementing guilds in an organization can have far-reaching effects on team dynamics and productivity. Guilds, through their inherent structure and alignment, foster an environment that emphasizes both collective learning and professional excellence.

For one, the existence of guilds can improve collaboration between team members. Because guilds are usually made up of people with similar interests or skills, they create a natural platform for knowledge sharing and collaboration. They also create a safe space where team members can share new ideas and develop creative solutions. In this way, guilds foster innovation and help teams work more creatively and efficiently.

On the other hand, guilds promote professional competence. By providing a framework for regular learning and development activities, they enable employees to continuously improve their skills and knowledge. This not only contributes to the personal development of each individual, but also increases the overall competence and productivity of the team.

Another significant aspect is identity and bonding within guilds. By creating a sense of belonging and community, guilds help improve employee retention and satisfaction. The shared interests and goals within a guild can help foster a strong sense of belonging and increase loyalty among team members.

Finally, guilds can help break down organizational silos. They promote exchange between different parts of the organization and can thus help improve transparency and understanding of the work of other teams. This, in turn, can help improve the overall productivity of the organization.

However, it is important to note that guild implementation must be carefully planned and managed to maximize its benefits. A poorly executed implementation could lead to confusion or resistance within the team. Therefore, it is essential to clearly communicate what guilds are, why they are being introduced, and what benefits they offer before implementation.

Taken as a whole, guilds, when used effectively, can be a powerful tool for improving team dynamics and productivity. They foster a culture of learning and collaboration, strengthen expertise, and help break down organizational silos. With careful planning and execution, they can be a key element in a company's organizational structure.

2.5 Squadron: structure and influence

In the context of the Spotify model, squadrons (in the original "squads") represent the smallest unit and are of great importance in terms of their structure and function. They primarily represent self-organized teams that work independently on specific projects or tasks. As the heart of the model, they are key to the agility and innovation that characterize Spotify as an organization.

Each squadron usually consists of six to twelve people and has a clear mission. The members of a squadron bring different skills and knowledge required to achieve their specific goals. For example, they include developers, designers, and product managers. This multidisciplinary composition enables effective collaboration and means that each squadron can, in principle, act autonomously.

Each squadron is headed by a squad lead, often a technical leader, who has a leadership role but does not necessarily make decisions. Instead, his job is to foster cooperation within the squadron and ensure that it is making progress toward its goals.

A key feature of squadrons is their autonomy. They have the freedom to make decisions and shape their ways of working based on what they think will be most effective. This autonomy is supported by the principle of "minimum viable bureaucracy," which states that only as much bureaucracy as necessary should be introduced.

But despite their autonomy, squadrons do not operate in a vacuum. Rather, they are part of a larger system in which they interact with other squadrons, tribes, and guilds. These interactions allow for information sharing and coordination between different parts of the organization, which contributes to overall efficiency and innovation.

The squadrons also have a significant impact on the culture and dynamics within the organization. Through their self-organization and autonomy, they foster a culture of ownership and innovation. They encourage employees to take initiative and develop creative solutions, which contributes to Spotify's innovative strength.

In addition, squadrons enable a fast and flexible response to change. Because each squadron sets its own working practices and priorities, it can respond quickly to new information or changes in the business environment. This flexibility is a key factor in Spotify's agility and competitiveness.

Overall, the squadron concept in the Spotify model represents a radical approach to organizational structure. It breaks with traditional hierarchies and instead promotes autonomy and personal responsibility. This has a significant impact on the way work is organized and performed, and helps to foster a dynamic and innovative culture.

Introduction to the structure and function of squadrons

Squadrons, or "squads" in English, are the smallest unit in the Spotify model and the building blocks that form the foundation of this innovative organizational model. Each squadron is an independent team consisting of six to twelve members and pursuing a specific mission.

The key role of a squadron is ownership. Each squadron is self-organized and autonomous in its decisions. This means that it has the freedom and responsibility to choose its own working methods, technologies and processes that best fit its specific mission.

Members of a squadron bring different skills and competencies to the table and work closely together to achieve common goals. A squadron may include developers, designers, testers, product managers, and other roles. This multidisciplinary composition enables the squadron to have all the necessary skills and knowledge to autonomously accomplish its mission.

Despite this autonomy, squadrons are not isolated. Rather, they are part of a larger whole and interact with other elements of the Spotify model such as tribes, guilds, and alliances. These interactions are important for sharing knowledge, coordinating activities, and fostering collaboration at the organizational level.

Each squadron is headed by a squad lead, a person who acts as a coach and supporter rather than a traditional manager. The squad lead is responsible for fostering cooperation within the squadron and creating the conditions under which the squadron can succeed. However, he or she does not make the operational decisions - that is the responsibility of the entire squadron.

Finally, squadrons have another important function in the Spotify model: they are key to fostering an innovative and agile culture. Through the self-organization and autonomy of squadrons, employees are encouraged to take initiative, experiment, and develop creative solutions. This contributes to the innovation and agility of the organization and makes the Spotify model an attractive approach for many companies seeking similar dynamism and creativity.

The role of squadrons in the Spotify model and how they interact with other elements

In the colorful palette of the Spotify model, squadrons play a crucial role as they are the driving force behind the work. Their structural flexibility and functional autonomy enable smooth execution of projects and initiate innovative solutions.

But squadrons do not stand alone. They are embedded in a network of tribes, guilds, and alliances that make up the entire ecosystem of the Spotify model. This dynamic interaction between elements strikes a balance between autonomy and collaboration that is at the core of the organization.

A squadron is typically part of a tribe, a larger organizational unit that includes multiple squadrons focused on similar or related tasks. The tribe provides an environment in which squadrons can interact, share ideas, and learn from each other. Coordination occurs within a tribe, facilitating the overlap and sharing of resources and ensuring a cohesive approach to achieving common goals.

In addition, members of squadrons interact across guilds. Guilds are cross-organizational communities of interest where professionals from different squadrons and tribes come together to share knowledge, exchange best practices, and improve their skills in a particular area. For example, a developer who is part of a squadron may also be a member of a guild focused on advancing programming languages.

By combining these horizontal and vertical interactions, the Spotify model forms a dynamic, adaptive network that offers the best of both worlds: the autonomy and flexibility of small, self-organized teams and the strength and stability of larger, structured organizational units. By aligning squadrons, tribes, and guilds, the model can make the most of individual skills and talents while ensuring a coordinated, focused effort. This balance between autonomy and interdependence is a key factor that makes the Spotify model both efficient and innovative.

Examples of the application of squadrons in organizations

The introduction of the squadron concept in organizational structure has taken root not only in the technology sector, but also in other industries. Here are some concise examples of how squadrons are being applied in various organizations.

Example 1: ABC Bank

ABC Bank, a Dutch multinational bank, has implemented squadrons as part of its comprehensive agile transformation. The bank has dissolved its traditional organizational structure and instead introduced squadrons, tribes and guilds. Each squadron focuses on a specific customer offering and consists of multidisciplinary teams, including product developers, IT specialists and commercial experts. This integrated approach enables squadrons to deliver complete products and services while maintaining a high degree of autonomy.

Example 2: BY

BY, a global provider of technology and services, uses squadrons to accelerate the development and delivery of software solutions. BY's squadrons are self-organized teams composed of developers, product owners, and scrum masters. They are responsible for delivering autonomous products or services from ideation to implementation. BY has found that adopting the squadron model has increased productivity and improved time-to-market.

Example 3: ZT Bank

ZT Bank, a British mobile bank, also has squadrons embedded in its organization. The bank is divided into different squadrons, each consisting of about ten people. Each squadron is responsible for a specific aspect of the business, such as user experience, payment infrastructure, or fraud prevention. This structure allows ZT Bank to respond quickly to market trends and deliver innovative features in a short time.

These examples show how the application of squadrons can help organizations improve speed, flexibility and customer centricity. By decentralizing decision making and encouraging ownership, squadrons can make a significant contribution to organizational performance.

Case studies of companies that have successfully deployed squadrons

One of the keys to understanding the Squadron model is to look at companies that have used it with success. Here are two in-depth case studies that show how different companies have implemented the model and the results they have achieved.

Case study 1: ABC Bank

ABC Bank began its agile journey in 2015 with the clear goal of putting its customers at the center of all its efforts. It decided to use the squadron structure to streamline its work processes and organizations.

For example, a squadron at ABC Bank focuses on mobile app development. It consists of various roles, including a product owner, front-end and back-end developers, UX designers, and IT specialists. Each member has a specific expertise and a clearly defined role, but works closely with the other team members to create an optimal customer experience.

Within two years of moving to the squadron model, ABC Bank saw significant improvements. Time-to-market for new features was significantly reduced, and customer touches increased by nearly 20%. The team also felt stronger alignment and motivation from a clear focus on customer needs and experience.

Case study 2: FFO

FFO, the Berlin-based online fashion retailer, began implementing the squadron model in 2015. With more than 200 squadrons within the organization, FFO wanted to increase autonomy, improve coordination and foster a culture of ownership.

One of FFO's squadrons focused on improving the checkout process has made remarkable progress in just one year. Through collaboration between product managers, software engineers, designers and data analysts in the squadron, FFO has significantly reduced the number of abandoned purchases and increased sales.

These case studies show how the squadron model works in practice and the positive impact it can have on companies. By implementing this model, ABC Bank and FFO were able to achieve their goals while increasing employee satisfaction and motivation.

The impact of using squadrons on team dynamics and productivity

The use of squadrons in the Spotify model has profound implications for team dynamics and productivity in organizations. By creating small, autonomous teams focused on specific product areas or services, squadrons can foster collaboration, improve communication, and ultimately increase efficiency. But how exactly does this happen? And how do squadrons affect individual and collective performance?

First, the squadron model fosters a culture of ownership. By giving each squadron full control over its product area, team members are encouraged to take ownership and make decisions that move the product forward. This responsibility can increase team member motivation and engagement and lead to higher productivity.

In addition, the squadron structure promotes better communication and collaboration. Because each squadron consists of a mix of roles and skills, team members rely on working closely together and communicating effectively to achieve their goals. This can lead to breaking down silos and encouraging the sharing of knowledge and ideas.

In addition, the squadron model can accelerate product development. By giving each squadron responsibility for its own product area, decisions can be made more quickly and products can be brought to market faster. This leads to improved time-to-market and can ultimately help increase a company's competitive advantage.

However, the use of squadrons can also bring challenges. It requires a significant change in corporate culture and ways of working. Teams must learn to work autonomously, and managers must learn to relinquish trust and control. This can initially lead to resistance and challenges. But with the right support and leadership, the squadron model can lead to improved team dynamics and productivity.

In summary, the squadron model can improve team dynamics and productivity by fostering ownership, collaboration and faster decision-making. However, as with any change, careful planning, implementation and alignment is required to ensure that the use of squadrons contributes to the success of the organization.

2.6 Chapters and their meaning

Introduction to the structure and function of chapters

Any good novel is divided into chapters that help the reader follow the plot and digest the story. Similarly, in the world of business organization, chapters help us manage and structure large tasks. At Spotify, the pioneer of the agile model we discuss here, chapters are a horizontal division of the organizational structure that brings together employees with similar skills or roles.

A chapter is typically led by a Chapter Lead, who is responsible for the technical direction and development of its chapter members. Chapter members might work in different squadrons and teams, but they share a common specialty or role that brings them together within the chapter.

In terms of structure, chapters are organized by subject area or role. For example, you could have a chapter for UI/UX design, backend development, or data analysis. The key element here is that members within a chapter have a similar expertise or role and can therefore share specific experience and knowledge.

In terms of function, chapters serve several important purposes. First, they provide an environment for continuous learning and professional development as members share experiences, learn from each other, and work together to improve their skills. Second, chapters create a community of employees who share similar roles and interests, which strengthens a sense of belonging and cohesion. Third, they help ensure consistent application of practices and processes across the organization by providing a forum for alignment and standardization of methods.

Just as chapters in a novel guide the reader through the story, chapters in an organization help structure and support employees' journey through their careers. They serve as anchor points for professional development, community building, and best practices, making them an integral part of an effective agile model.

The role of chapters in the Spotify model and their interaction with other elements

In the Spotify agile model, chapters play a central role. They are the home base for all professionals in a given discipline, regardless of which squadrons they work in. Chapters act as silos of expertise while enabling a constant exchange of knowledge and best practices within their domain. In this regard, the chapter leader acts not only as an administrator, but also as a mentor who promotes the personal and professional development of his or her chapter members.

In terms of interaction with other elements of the Spotify model, particularly squadrons and guilds, chapters are best understood as cross-cutting organizations. Whereas a squadron focuses on a specific product or service and is made up of various professionals, a chapter focuses on a specific discipline. A front-end developer, for example, could be a member of a squadron working on a specific app, but could also be part of a chapter of all front-end developers in the company.

Chapters and squadrons thus interact in a way that provides a balance of professional excellence and product focus. While working in squadrons helps achieve specific product goals, belonging to a chapter provides a community of professionals in which to learn from the experiences of others and develop in one's role.

By comparison, guilds are more informal, interest-based groups that can span roles and disciplines. They provide a space for sharing ideas and learning new skills that are not necessarily directly related to an employee's role. Although membership in a guild is optional, they complement the more formal structures of chapters and squadrons by providing an additional layer of networking and learning.

Overall, chapters combined with squadrons and guilds allow for a high degree of flexibility and adaptability, while fostering a strong cultural identity and creating an environment that supports both individual employee development and the achievement of corporate goals.

Examples of the application of chapters in organizations

Chapters provide an opportunity to deepen expertise in specific areas while promoting effective sharing of knowledge and best practices within the organization. Here are some examples of how companies have successfully embedded chapters into their organizational structure:

Example 1: ABC Bank

ABC Bank, a Dutch financial services provider, is using the Spotify model to support its agile transformation. They have introduced chapters into their organizational structure to group employees with similar skill sets. Within these chapters, they encourage professional development and promote collaboration to enable continuous learning and sharing of best practices.

Example 2: BY

BY, the world's leading provider of technology and service solutions, has also integrated chapters into its organizational structure. In their chapters, engineers, data analysts or marketing experts come together to share their expertise and learn from each other. The chapters help to maintain technical standards and improve the quality of work.

Example 3: FFO

FFO, the European online fashion retailer, also uses chapters to pool expertise and promote collaboration. Their "Performance Marketing" chapter, for example, focuses on specific aspects of online marketing. Within this chapter, members share ideas and develop strategies to improve their marketing practices.

These examples show that the chapter structure is not only used in technology companies or start-ups, but also in more traditional sectors such as banking and manufacturing. Regardless of the type of company, embedding chapters in the organizational structure promotes knowledge sharing and employee professional development.

Case studies of companies that have successfully used chapters

In practice, we can find numerous examples of how companies have integrated chapters into their organization and achieved significant benefits as a result. A few detailed case studies will illustrate this.

Case study 1: ABC Bank

ABC Bank, based in the Netherlands, has undergone a significant transformation in its organizational structure in recent years. Chapters played a crucial role in the implementation of the Spotify model. In this structure, ABC employees with similar areas of expertise were grouped into chapters led by a chapter leader. This chapter leader was responsible not only for staff development, but also for ensuring that knowledge and best practices were shared within the chapter.

One of the main benefits of this structure was improved communication and collaboration. Employees felt encouraged to share ideas and work on improving processes and tools. The introduction of chapters helped transform ABC Bank into a learning organization where continuous improvement and innovation are encouraged.

Case study 2: FFO

FFO, the European online fashion retailer, is another company that has successfully implemented chapters. Chapters at FFO were introduced to promote the professional development of employees and facilitate the exchange of best practices.

One outstanding example is the "Performance Marketing" chapter. Here, specialists with a passion for data-driven marketing were brought together. Regular collaboration and sharing within the chapter led to improvements in the company's marketing strategies and tactics. The chapter helped members deepen their skills while directly contributing to the company's performance.

These case studies illustrate how chapters can help foster a culture of learning and continuous improvement. By grouping employees with similar expertise and encouraging them to share knowledge and best practices, companies can foster innovation and improve the quality of their work.

The impact of using chapters on team dynamics and productivity.

The implementation of chapters in the organizational structure of a company has a significant impact on the dynamics within teams and their productivity. The following are some of the most significant impacts.

Strengthening of professional competence

Chapters create a platform for sharing expertise and best practices. This shared learning environment strengthens the professional skills of team members and enables them to perform their work at a higher level. As a result, teams can work more effectively and efficiently and achieve higher quality standards.

Promoting cooperation

Collaboration within a chapter positively promotes team dynamics. Because members of a chapter share similar expertise and interests, they often develop a stronger bond and sense of belonging. This dynamic can lead to higher motivation and improved teamwork.

Enabling faster problem resolution

By sharing knowledge and experience within a chapter, team members can respond more quickly to challenges and solve problems more efficiently. When a member encounters an obstacle, they can draw on the collective knowledge of the chapter to find a solution. This collective problem solving leads to faster decision making and increases overall productivity.

Increasing the capacity for innovation

Chapters also foster innovation. As team members are encouraged to share ideas and new approaches within the chapter, an environment is created where creativity and innovation can flourish. This innovative culture can lead to breakthrough ideas and improvements in work processes that ultimately increase productivity.

In summary, chapters can have a significant impact on team dynamics and productivity. By strengthening technical expertise, fostering collaboration, accelerating problem solving, and increasing innovation, chapters can help boost team performance and a company's overall productivity.

2.7 Success stories and case studies

Detailed case study of an organization that has successfully implemented the Spotify model

Let's look at a detailed case study that demonstrates the successful deployment of the Spotify model in practice. The organization in this scenario is a global technology company called "TechForward" that specializes in developing innovative software solutions.

The initial situation

TechForward has always faced challenges in scaling its work processes. With an increasing number of projects and employees in different countries, the traditional organizational model was reaching its limits. Communication barriers, unclear responsibilities, and a lack of focus on product development were just some of the problems.

The implementation of the Spotify model

To overcome these difficulties, TechForward decided to implement the Spotify model. The organization was divided into Squads, Tribes, Chapters and Guilds. Each Squad was given a clear mission and responsibility for a specific product or product function. Squads were grouped into larger Tribes that interacted closely with each other.

Chapters were formed on the basis of expertise, with each chapter having a Chapter Lead who was responsible for the professional development of members. Guilds, as interdisciplinary communities, served to share knowledge on specific topics across the company.

The effects

TechForward's implementation of the Spotify model brought significant improvements.

Increased product focus: Each squad had clear product responsibility, resulting in a higher focus on product development. With independent, cross-functional teams, TechForward was able to accelerate product development and better align products with customer needs.

More efficient communication: The clear division into squads and tribes improved communication and collaboration within teams. It became easier to share information and make joint decisions.

Professional growth: The structure in chapters enabled a stronger focus on professional development. Employees were able to develop within their area of expertise and learn from the expertise of their colleagues.

Innovation and creativity: The Guilds promoted the exchange of knowledge and ideas across teams, which led to increased innovation in the company.

Overall, TechForward has achieved significant improvement in productivity, team dynamics, and the quality of its products by implementing the Spotify model. It turns out that this model, properly applied, can have a significant positive impact on the work processes in an organization.

Description of the challenges and how they were overcome

The implementation of the Spotify model at TechForward was by no means a seamless process, but presented a number of challenges. One of the first and biggest stumbling blocks was the initial skepticism and resistance of some employees to the radical change.

Resistance to change

Many employees were used to the traditional hierarchical structure and perceived the Spotify model as uncertain and chaotic. They feared that the new structure would lead to misunderstandings and conflicts. To overcome this resistance, TechForward invested significantly in change management and internal communications. They organized workshops and information sessions to introduce the model to employees and explain the benefits.

Building cross-functional teams

Another challenge was staffing the squads with the right skills. TechForward needed a mix of developers, designers, testers and product managers in each squad. Finding the right people for each team wasn't always easy. But through consistent staff development and targeted recruiting, they were able to overcome this hurdle as well.

Communication between the teams

Communication and coordination between the various teams also presented a challenge. Despite clear roles and responsibilities, there was friction and ambiguity at the beginning. To resolve this, TechForward relied on regular meetings and check-ins between the teams and promoted the exchange of information through tools and platforms.

Adaptation of the corporate culture

Perhaps the biggest challenge was adapting the company culture to the Spotify model. TechForward had to foster a culture of ownership and continuous learning to truly bring the model to life. This required time, patience, and the commitment of leaders at all levels.

Ultimately, TechForward was able to successfully overcome these challenges and create an effective, efficient, and dynamic work environment based on the Spotify model. This process required courage, perseverance, and a willingness to challenge conventional methods and break new ground.

Analysis of the impact of the implementation of the Spotify model on the organization

The introduction of the Spotify model at TechForward had a profound impact on the company. It not only changed the way they work, but also the culture and face of the organization.

Increased productivity and efficiency

One of the most notable effects was a significant improvement in productivity. The introduction of squads, each organized around a product or function, enabled more focused and efficient work. Each squad was able to focus fully on its specific goals, resulting in faster development cycles and higher quality work results.

Promotion of personal responsibility and creativity

In addition, the Spotify model led to a culture of ownership and innovation. Employees felt empowered and motivated by the autonomy given to them through the squad structure. This led to higher employee satisfaction and an explosion of creativity and innovation in the organization.

Improved collaboration and communication

The implementation of squadrons and chapters also improved collaboration and communication within the company. The flat hierarchy and constant interaction between teams promoted open and transparent communication. It also fostered collaboration between different teams, which led to better solution finding and improved working relationships.

Improvement of the ability to learn and adapt

In addition, TechForward's implementation of the Spotify model greatly improved its ability to learn and adapt. The structure of the model fostered an environment of continuous learning and improvement. This enabled TechForward to respond to changes and challenges more quickly and effectively.

In summary, implementing the Spotify model at TechForward has transformed the organization. It has increased productivity and efficiency, fostered a culture of ownership and creativity, improved collaboration and communication, and strengthened the company's ability to learn and adapt. It is clear that the Spotify model has had a significant impact on TechForward and plays a key role in their continued success.

Detailed case study of another organization that has successfully implemented the Spotify model

Let's take a closer look at InnovativeSoft, an emerging tech company specializing in educational technology software development. InnovativeSoft had about 300 employees and was facing many challenges, including inefficient communication, lack of innovation, and poor responsiveness to market changes. The management team recognized that change was needed and decided to implement the Spotify model.

Implementation of the Spotify model at InnovativeSoft

SPOTIFY MODEL: PRACTICAL IMPLEMENTATION GUIDE

The implementation of the Spotify model began with a thorough organizational analysis. The management team identified key areas where changes needed to be made and set goals and expectations for the transition. Employees were then divided into squads, each focused on a specific product line or function. Each squad was self-organized and responsible for planning, developing and implementing its projects.

In addition to the squads, chapters were formed, which were cross-functional groups of professionals working in similar areas. The chapters served as a platform for knowledge sharing and professional development. Furthermore, a leadership system was implemented in which squad and chapter leaders acted as servant leaders, supporting and empowering their teams rather than commanding them.

Challenges and how to overcome them

Implementing the Spotify model at InnovativeSoft was not without its challenges. One of the biggest challenges was resistance to the changes from some employees. To overcome this, management conducted extensive training and workshops to promote understanding and acceptance of the new model. In addition, employees were given the opportunity to provide feedback and participate in the design of the new structure, which helped to strengthen the sense of ownership and acceptance.

Another challenge was managing the autonomous squads and ensuring they worked together effectively. To achieve this, InnovativeSoft implemented Agile practices such as Daily Stand-ups and Retrospectives, which helped improve communication and coordination between the teams.

Successful results of the implementation

The implementation of the Spotify model led to remarkable changes at InnovativeSoft. Productivity increased as squads were able to fully focus on their specific tasks. In addition, squad autonomy and servant leadership led to increased employee satisfaction and a more dynamic, innovative culture.

Internal communication also improved significantly. By introducing chapters and implementing Agile practices, employees were able to communicate and collaborate more effectively. This led to better solutions and higher quality products.

Overall, implementing the Spotify model helped InnovativeSoft become a more agile, innovative, and productive company. It enabled them to adapt more quickly to market changes and strengthen their competitive position. InnovativeSoft is an excellent example of how implementing the Spotify model can lead to significant improvements and success.

Description of the challenges and how they were overcome

InnovativeSoft, like any organization, faced a number of challenges in implementing the Spotify model. It is important to note that any business transformation will inevitably face some resistance. This is human nature, as we are creatures of habit and often perceive change as a threat.

One of the first and biggest challenges was the lack of acceptance among some employees. This skepticism was not necessarily a rejection of the new model, but rather a natural reaction to change, especially when it has a significant impact on the way people are used to working. To overcome this challenge, InnovativeSoft focused on transparency and communication. Employees were involved in the change process from the beginning, their concerns were heard, and regular information and training sessions were held. This open communication helped increase understanding and acceptance of the new model.

Another challenge was coordination and collaboration within and between squads. Because the squads were largely autonomous, there were concerns about consistency and quality of work. InnovativeSoft addressed this challenge by implementing Agile methods such as daily stand-ups and retrospectives. These methods ensured that the teams were on track, fostered communication, and allowed them to continuously learn and improve.

The transition to the Servant Leadership model was also a challenge. Many leaders were used to top-down management and needed to learn how to effectively fill their roles in this new model. InnovativeSoft solved this problem by providing training and coaching where leaders learned the principles and practices of Servant Leadership. This enabled them to embrace the new roles and effectively support the teams.

Finally, the transition to the Spotify model was not a one-time event, but a continuous process. InnovativeSoft had to learn to be flexible and open to change, and to constantly evaluate and adapt. This was helped by the Spotify model itself, which encourages experimentation and continuous learning. InnovativeSoft employees learned to adapt the model to their specific needs and constantly improve it on their journey to agility.

Analysis of the impact of the implementation of the Spotify model on the organization

InnovativeSoft, like many organizations, was characterized by a culture of bureaucracy and hierarchy before adopting the Spotify model. However, the transformation had a far-reaching impact on the organization, both in terms of team dynamics and productivity.

First, the organization experienced a significant shift in the way teams worked together. Through the implementation of Squads, Tribes, Chapters and Guilds, communication and collaboration within and between teams was much more direct and effective. A stronger sense of belonging and ownership was fostered among employees as they had more autonomy and influence over their work. This change also led to increased employee satisfaction and motivation, which had a positive impact on productivity.

Second, the Spotify model has strengthened InnovativeSoft's innovative power. The ability to experiment autonomously and implement ideas quickly has been a big step toward a culture of innovation. It has unlocked the potential that lies within each and every employee and has positioned the company to quickly adapt to and even drive change.

Third, the role of leaders within the organization has changed significantly. They moved from a hierarchical model to a "servant leadership" model, where they help teams achieve their goals rather than giving instructions from the top. This change has had a profound effect on InnovativeSoft's culture, fostering an atmosphere of trust and collaboration.

In addition, the Spotify model has helped InnovativeSoft become more competitive. By responding quickly and flexibly to market changes, the company was better able to meet customer needs and hold its own against its competitors. This led to an improved market position and ultimately to increased sales.

Ultimately, InnovativeSoft's experience shows that adopting the Spotify model, while fraught with challenges, can have a number of positive impacts on an organization. It can change culture, increase productivity, strengthen innovation and improve competitiveness. However, it is important to emphasize that the Spotify model is not a "one-size-fits-all" approach and that each organization must adapt it to its specific needs and circumstances.

Part 3: Implementing the Spotify model in your company

3.1 Assessment of company culture and identification of need for change

An organization's culture is an integral part of its identity and shapes everything from work processes to employee retention. That's why assessing corporate culture is a critical first step in recognizing the need for change and identifying opportunities for improvement.

Assessing corporate culture is a multi-faceted task. It is not only about understanding the existing business climate, but also about exploring the deeper values and norms that shape behavior and decisions within the organization. One can assess culture through various methods, such as employee surveys, observation of behaviors, or even formal cultural audits.

An important dimension to consider in a culture assessment is openness to change and innovation. How does the organization respond to new ideas? Is the environment conducive to experimentation and risk-taking? In an agile environment, such as the Spotify model promotes, it is critical to have a culture that welcomes and supports change.

Another critical aspect is the evaluation of hierarchical levels and decision-making processes. Are decisions centralized or decentralized? How are opinions and feedback from employees taken into account? The Spotify model places great emphasis on autonomy and participation, so there could be a need for change here if the existing culture is strongly hierarchical.

Assessing collaboration and communication is also critical. How do teams work together? Are there barriers that prevent effective collaboration and communication? The Spotify model emphasizes close collaboration and open communication, and any barriers in this area would need to be addressed.

Ultimately, the goal of the culture assessment is to gain a clear understanding of the prevailing culture and identify areas that need improvement for successful implementation of the Spotify model. Through this understanding, the organization can develop targeted strategies to achieve greater alignment with the agile principles that are at the heart of the Spotify model.

How to evaluate the current company culture

Assessing the current corporate culture is a complex and multi-faceted task that requires a careful approach. At its core, it is about understanding the current state of affairs, uncovering the invisible norms and values that guide behavior within the organization, and in this way identifying areas that may require improvement.

First of all, it is helpful to use various sources of information to gain a comprehensive picture of the culture. These can be formal documents such as corporate mission statements or employee handbooks, but also informal channels such as employee interviews or observations of daily working life.

One method that has proven particularly effective is conducting employee surveys. These can be designed in a variety of ways, from anonymous online surveys to personal interviews. Important areas that should be covered in such surveys are general job satisfaction, perceptions of corporate values, cooperation between teams, and attitudes toward change and innovation.

Another useful tool for assessing company culture is observation. By observing how employees interact, how decisions are made, or how conflicts are resolved, one can learn a lot about the prevailing norms and values. Observations can be done in an informal way, for example, by attending meetings or observing everyday work, or in a formal way, for example, through structured observation studies.

In addition, analyzing existing data from HR departments can be informative. Data on employee turnover, sick days or the result of employee evaluations can provide indications of the working atmosphere and possible problem areas.

Another approach is to conduct a cultural audit. This is a systematic examination of the various aspects of the company's culture, including prevailing values and beliefs, communication styles, and leadership practices. A cultural audit can be very revealing, but it also requires careful planning and execution.

Ultimately, the assessment of the company culture should involve a combination of different methods in order to obtain as comprehensive and accurate a picture as possible. It is important to keep emphasizing that the aim is not to make a final judgment, but to gain a better understanding of the culture so that improvements can be made on this basis.

Identify the changes needed to implement the Spotify model.

Implementing the Spotify model in an organization requires a deep understanding of the existing culture and the changes required to pave the way for the new ways of working.

The first necessary change concerns the organizational structure. The Spotify model involves the creation of smaller, cross-functional teams, known as squads, which work autonomously and bear responsibility for specific projects or product areas. This means that traditional hierarchical structures based on strict command and control mechanisms must be dismantled and replaced by more flexible and dynamic structures. The aim here is to achieve a flatter hierarchy that enables decentralized decision-making.

The second point is to create an agile culture. Agile practices, as embodied in the Spotify model, require a high degree of flexibility, responsiveness, and openness to change. This may mean rethinking traditional project management methods that focus on detailed planning and tight control and replacing them with more agile approaches.

A third important aspect is skills training and development. The introduction of the Spotify model requires not only new working methods, but also new competencies and skills among employees. For example, team members need to be able to work autonomously and on their own responsibility, and managers need to adapt to seeing their role more as coaches and supporters than controllers. Therefore, a comprehensive training and development program should be implemented to ensure that all stakeholders acquire the necessary skills and knowledge.

Last but not least, it is crucial to provide the necessary technological infrastructures. The Spotify model relies on technologies and tools that support efficient collaboration, communication and documentation. This may mean upgrading existing systems or introducing new ones to ensure smooth implementation of the model.

Identifying and making these changes is not a simple process and requires a long-term, strategic approach. It is important to emphasize that the Spotify model is not a one-size-fits-all organization. Each organization must adapt the model to its specific needs, taking into account the unique aspects of its culture.

Case studies and examples of adapting company culture to the Spotify model

Let's start with the case study of TechSoft, a software development company that decided to implement the Spotify model to increase its agility and productivity. TechSoft was previously highly hierarchical and had an ingrained command-and-control culture.

To adopt the Spotify model, TechSoft had to radically change its organization. The first steps included the introduction of squads, tribes and chapters to encourage collaboration and information sharing. This restructuring was done gradually and transparently, with regular communication and feedback sessions to address concerns and drive adoption.

In parallel, a comprehensive training program was introduced to provide the necessary skills for working in squads and tribes and to train managers in their new role as servant leaders. TechSoft also emphasized building a culture of trust and ownership by introducing transparent performance measurements and feedback mechanisms and encouraging employees to take initiative and responsibility.

Another example is HealthPlus, a healthcare provider that implemented the Spotify model to drive its digital transformation. HealthPlus was in a traditional, bureaucratic culture that inhibited the company's ability to innovate and respond.

HealthPlus began its transformation process with a thorough analysis of its existing culture and processes. The company then launched several pilot projects to test the Spotify model in specific areas and identify the necessary adjustments. This incremental approach enabled HealthPlus to gain key insights and gradually roll out the model across the organization.

A key element of HealthPlus' transformation was the promotion of an agile culture. This was achieved by introducing agile practices such as Scrum and Kanban, conducting regular retrospectives, and fostering a continuous improvement mindset. In addition, HealthPlus provided the necessary tools and infrastructure to support collaboration and the agile way of working.

These case studies show that adapting the company culture to the Spotify model is a complex and multi-layered task that requires careful planning and continuous adjustments. Nevertheless, the benefits in terms of increased agility, productivity and employee satisfaction are significant and justify the effort.

3.2 Strategies for switching to the Spotify model

SPOTIFY MODEL: PRACTICAL IMPLEMENTATION GUIDE

Moving to the Spotify model is a profound change that must be well thought out and carefully planned. Below are some strategies that have proven effective in making this transition smooth and successful.

Understand the model: The first step in moving to the Spotify model is to understand it thoroughly. The model is more than just a new organizational structure - it's a new way of working based on autonomy, ownership and collaboration. It is important that all members of the organization, from managers to individual employees, understand the model and recognize its benefits.

Assess your current culture: Before making any changes, you need to understand where you are. Conduct a thorough assessment of your current culture to identify strengths and weaknesses and areas where change is needed. This can be done through surveys, interviews, workshops or other methods.

Develop a transformation plan: Based on your culture assessment, you should develop a detailed plan for transitioning to the Spotify model. This plan should clearly define what changes will be made, how they will be implemented, and who will be responsible. The plan should also include milestones and success criteria to measure and monitor progress.

Introduce changes gradually: A radical shift to the Spotify model can lead to resistance and unrest. Instead, introduce changes incrementally, starting with small pilots to test the model and identify necessary adjustments. In this way, you can gain valuable insights and drive acceptance of the model before rolling it out across the organization.

Training and support: The introduction of the Spotify model requires new skills and ways of thinking. A comprehensive training and support program is therefore essential to equip employees with the necessary skills and prepare them for their new roles. This can include training on agile methodologies, workshops on topics such as ownership and collaboration, and coaching for managers.

Communication and transparency: Moving to the Spotify model is a major change that can raise questions and concerns. Open and transparent communication is therefore critical to avoid mistrust and encourage adoption. Keep employees informed of progress, answer their questions, and take their feedback on board.

Encourage feedback and continuous improvement: One of the core principles of the Spotify model is continuous improvement. Encourage employees to share their feedback and identify opportunities for improvement. Conduct regular retrospectives to reflect on what has been learned and develop actions for improvement.

Foster culture: Moving to the Spotify model requires a culture of trust, ownership, and collaboration. Strive to promote these values in your organization by, for example, introducing transparent performance measurements and feedback mechanisms and encouraging employees to take initiative and responsibility.

Moving to the Spotify model is no easy feat, but with the right preparation, strategy, and execution, it can lead to a transformation that makes your organization more agile, productive, and future-ready.

Overview of the main steps to implement the Spotify model

Implementing the Spotify model is a multi-step journey that goes far beyond mere structural change. It requires transformation at multiple levels, from culture to processes to mindset. The following outlines the key steps required to successfully implement this model.

SPOTIFY MODEL: PRACTICAL IMPLEMENTATION GUIDE

1. Form a leadership team: The first step is to form a dedicated leadership team to guide the transformation. This team should include both executives and key employees and should clearly define and communicate the vision, values and goals of the transformation.

2. training and education: A basic understanding of the Spotify model and its principles is essential for successful implementation. It is important that all employees, from top management to individual team members, are trained and educated to understand what the model is, how it works, and the benefits it offers.

3. evaluation of the current organization: Before changes are made, the current organizational structure, processes and culture should be carefully evaluated. This will help identify potential barriers to implementation and areas where specific adjustments are needed.

4. preparation of an implementation plan: Based on the assessment, a detailed implementation plan should be developed. This plan should clearly define what changes are necessary, how they will be implemented, and who is responsible for them. It should also include milestones and metrics to measure success.

5. Conduct pilot projects: Rather than rolling out the Spotify model across the entire organization in one fell swoop, it can be helpful to run smaller pilot projects first. These pilot projects can provide valuable insights and help adapt the model to the specific needs and challenges of the organization.

6. incremental introduction: Based on the findings from the pilot projects, the Spotify model should be introduced gradually throughout the organization. This approach makes it possible to identify and address any challenges that may arise at an early stage.

7. Ongoing assessment and adaptation: Implementing the Spotify model is not a one-time process, but an ongoing journey. It is important to conduct regular assessments and continuously adapt the model to ensure it is working effectively and meeting the changing needs of the organization.

8. cultivating culture: Finally, culture plays a critical role in implementing the Spotify model. It is necessary to foster and nurture a culture of autonomy, trust, collaboration, and continuous improvement.

Moving to the Spotify model takes time, commitment and adaptability. But if these steps are followed, it can lead to a more powerful, agile and innovative organization.

Planning and timing for the changeover

Successfully implementing the Spotify model requires careful planning and timing. Since every organization is unique, there is no universal timeline that fits all. However, there are some basic considerations that can be helpful in creating a customized roadmap.

Evaluation Phase: In this phase, you should evaluate and understand your current organizational structure, culture and processes. This involves diving into the inner workings of your organization and conducting interviews, surveys and workshops. Depending on the size and complexity of your organization, this phase could take anywhere from a few weeks to a few months.

Planning phase: Based on the findings from the evaluation phase, you should create a detailed implementation plan. This should clarify the changes you need to make, the specific steps you will take to implement those changes, and the responsibilities of each member of your team.

The length of this phase will depend on the size of your organization and the complexity of the changes you need to make, but plan on at least one to two months.

Pilot: The pilot phase is an opportunity to test the Spotify model on a smaller scale before rolling it out to the entire organization. Select a small, representative team or department to implement the model and gather valuable feedback and insights. This phase could last from a few months to a year, depending on the results and adjustments that need to be made.

Roll-out phase: Based on the learnings from the pilot phase, you can start rolling out the Spotify model to the entire organization. This process should be gradual and incremental to ensure that each team has enough time to adapt to the new model. Depending on the size and structure of your organization, this roll-out could take anywhere from several months to several years.

Evaluation and adaptation phase: Finally, it is important to understand that the implementation of the Spotify model is a continuous process. You should regularly evaluate how the model is working and whether adjustments are needed. This should be considered an ongoing process that runs in parallel with the other phases.

These phases are, of course, guidelines, and actual implementation will vary depending on the specific circumstances of your organization. It is important to remain flexible and be prepared to adjust plans to respond to unexpected challenges or changes. In the end, the key to successful implementation of the Spotify model is patience, commitment, and a willingness to learn and adapt.

Strategies for overcoming challenges during transition

Moving to the Spotify model is a challenging task that requires both forward planning and a high degree of flexibility. Below are some strategies for addressing the typical challenges that may arise during this process.

Communication is key: One of the biggest challenges in implementing the Spotify model is communication. The changes that the Spotify model brings can be confusing and unsettling for employees. Therefore, clear, transparent and regular communication is essential. You should clearly explain the purpose and benefits of the transition and encourage an open dialogue with your employees. Provide regular updates on the progress of the project and actively seek feedback.

Continuous learning and adaptation: The Spotify model is not a fixed standard, but an agile and flexible model. It is important that your organization is willing to continuously learn and adapt. This may mean changing your plans based on feedback, experience, and new insights. Foster a culture of continuous improvement and experimentation.

Leadership support: Leaders play a critical role in implementing the Spotify model. They must not only understand and support the model, but also serve as role models and exemplify the new ways of working. Make sure your leaders have the training and support they need to take on this role effectively.

Involving all employees: The Spotify model affects all aspects of the organization, from team structure to work processes to corporate culture. It is therefore important that all employees are involved in the process. This can be done through workshops, surveys, feedback sessions and other participation mechanisms.

Patience and perseverance: Implementing the Spotify model is a long-term process that requires time and perseverance. It's important to have realistic expectations and not expect too much too quickly. Encourage your employees to see the process as a journey and celebrate the small successes along the way.

Each organization is unique and will have its own specific challenges in transitioning to the Spotify model. It's important to view these challenges not as obstacles, but as learning opportunities. With the right mindset, the right strategies, and the support of your employees, you can overcome these challenges and put your organization on the path to greater agility and innovation.

———————

3.3 Communication strategies to accompany the change process

The role of communication in change processes is crucial. It provides the framework within which information is shared, concerns are addressed, and a collective understanding is created. When implementing the Spotify model, clear and effective communication is essential to ensure a smooth and successful transition. This chapter presents several communication strategies that can help you achieve this.

1. clarity and transparency in communication

One of the most important strategies is transparent and clear communication about the change process. It is important that all stakeholders understand exactly what the transition to the Spotify model means, why it is happening, how it will proceed, and what impact it will have on day-to-day work. This can be achieved through regular updates, staff meetings, newsletters and other communication channels.

2. involvement of the managers

Managers play a central role in communicating change. They are often the ones who initiate and lead the change process, and they are also the ones who must communicate it to employees. It is important that leaders fully understand and commit to the Spotify model and the process of implementing it. They must be able to communicate the benefits of the model and address any concerns employees may have.

3. promote dialogue

One-way communication is not enough. It is important to foster a dialog between managers and employees. This can be achieved through regular feedback sessions, surveys and open discussions. Open dialogue allows concerns to be raised and solutions to be found, and helps to create a common understanding and direction.

4. adaptation of communication to different target groups

Different groups of employees may have different needs and expectations when it comes to communication. Some employees may need more technical details, while others may be more interested in the overall goals and benefits of the Spotify model. An effective communication strategy must take these differences into account and adjust communications accordingly.

5. use of different communication channels

There are many different ways to communicate information and it is important to choose the right channels. Emails, employee meetings, newsletters, intranet, social media and face-to-face meetings are just some of the possible communication channels. Choosing the right channels depends on several factors, such as the type of information to be communicated, employee preferences, and the size and structure of the organization.

6. regular communication

Implementing the Spotify model is a long-term process and it is important that communication about this process is regular. Regular updates on progress, upcoming steps and achievements can help maintain employee engagement and motivation.

By applying these strategies and encouraging open, honest, and regular communication about the change process, you can help reduce resistance, promote engagement, and achieve successful implementation of the Spotify model. It is important to keep in mind that communication strategies must be customized to meet the specific needs and challenges of your organization.

Important points for communication during the changeover

The transition to the Spotify model is a process that requires careful planning and execution. Communication is a key element of this process and how information is shared can have a significant impact on the success of the transition. Below are some key aspects to consider when communicating during this transition process:

1. simple and clear messages

Complex information about switching to the Spotify model should be presented in simple and easy-to-understand language. Unclear messages can lead to confusion and misunderstanding. It is therefore important to formulate clear and consistent messages that highlight the most important points of the changeover.

2. managers as communicators

Managers have a significant influence on the way change is perceived. They should act as role models and actively support the transition. Managers should also be able to clearly communicate the reasons for the change and the associated benefits.

3. regular updates

It is important to provide regular updates on the progress of the transition. This helps maintain transparency and builds trust in the process. It also shows employees that progress is being made and that their efforts are bearing fruit.

4. involvement of employees

Involving employees in the communication process can help increase engagement and minimize resistance. This can be achieved through regular feedback sessions, discussions and workshops. It is important that employees feel that their opinions are heard and valued.

5. adaptation of communication

Communication should be adapted to the different needs and preferences of employees. This may mean using different communication channels and formats to ensure that the message reaches and is understood by all.

6. highlighting the advantages

Communication should not only focus on the technical aspects of the changeover, but also highlight the benefits of the changeover. This can help to promote employee commitment and motivation.

Overall, it is important that communications during the transition to the Spotify model are carefully planned and executed to ensure that all stakeholders are informed and engaged. The points above can help develop and implement an effective communication strategy.

Development of effective communication channels and processes

Successfully transitioning to the Spotify model is a process that requires clear and effective communication. One of the challenges is to develop the right channels and processes for this communication. Below are some steps to develop effective communication channels and processes.

1. determination of the target groups

First, it is important to identify the different audiences within the organization that need to be informed about the transition to the Spotify model. These could be executives, project managers, team members, stakeholders, and others. Each of these groups may have different information needs and preferences.

2. selection of communication channels

Different communication channels can be suitable for different purposes and target groups. Some channels could be emails, intranet, meetings, newsletters, social media platforms, webinars or workshops. It is important to find the right mix that maximizes reach and reaches target audiences in the most effective way.

3. determination of the communication frequency

It is critical to set an appropriate frequency for communication. Too much communication can be seen as disruptive, while too little communication can lead to uncertainty and rumors. A good rule might be to give regular updates, but also when important milestones are reached or changes are made.

4. development of a message matrix

A message matrix can help to keep track of the different messages to be sent to the different target groups. This matrix could contain information about what is to be communicated, who the target group is, which channel is to be used and when the communication is to take place.

5. establishment of feedback loops

Feedback is an essential part of an effective communication process. It is therefore important to establish mechanisms to collect and respond to feedback from employees. This could include surveys, feedback sessions or other methods.

6. evaluation and adaptation

Finally, the communications strategy should be regularly reviewed and adjusted to ensure that it is effective. This could include measuring the reach and impact of communications, incorporating feedback, and making changes as needed.

By considering these points, organizations can develop effective communication channels and processes to inform employees about the shift to the Spotify model and help them along the path to implementation.

Case studies and examples of successful communication strategies

Implementing the Spotify model is a big step that requires targeted and careful communication. Here are some examples and case studies that represent successful communication strategies during such significant changes.

Case study 1: ABC Bank

ABC, a Dutch multinational bank, introduced a radical change in the way they work, based heavily on the Spotify model. To ensure that this change was understood and accepted by the entire organization, they relied on a comprehensive communication strategy.

The bank used a range of channels, including email bulletins, internal social media platforms and regular townhall meetings. However, the main part of the communication strategy consisted of in-depth workshops and training sessions for all employees. The trainings were specific to the needs of different departments and teams and were delivered by experts in the Spotify model. This strategy allowed ABC to ensure that the message about the change was communicated clearly and consistently.

Case study 2: ZT Software

ZT Software, a small IT company, decided to implement the Spotify model to effectively manage their growing teams. They used a range of communication strategies to inform the entire company about the upcoming changes.

One effective communication channel was the use of a corporate blog. In this, managers regularly published articles about the changes, progress and challenges of implementing the Spotify model. These regular updates not only provided transparency, but also gave employees the opportunity to ask questions and provide feedback. This fostered a culture of dialogue and openness throughout the change process.

Example: Weekly Huddles

Another effective communication strategy used in the transition to the Spotify model is regular "huddles." A huddle is a short, stand-up meeting held once a week to share updates, challenges and successes. These huddles allow teams to stay informed and respond quickly to issues as they arise. They also create a platform for transparency and collaboration.

These case studies and examples show that there are many different ways and options to ensure successful communication during the transition to the Spotify model. The key is to choose the right strategies, tailored to the specific needs and structures of your own company.

3.4 Selection criteria and training procedures for team members

At the heart of the Spotify model is the team, or more precisely, the so-called squads. A squad is an autonomous unit with a clear mission that operates with a high degree of autonomy and responsibility. This is a significant departure from more traditional corporate structures and requires thorough selection and training of team members. In this section, we will look at the criteria for selecting team members and how to design the training processes.

Selection criteria

The selection of team members is critical to the success of the Spotify model. The ideal candidates should have the following characteristics:

● Ownership: In the Spotify model, ownership is central. Team members must be able to organize and prioritize their work themselves, and they must be willing to take responsibility for their decisions and actions.

● Ability to collaborate: Since teamwork is the main focus, it is important that team members can communicate and collaborate well. They must be open to the ideas and suggestions of others and willing to share their knowledge and experience.

● Willingness to learn: In the Spotify model, team members are expected to constantly learn and develop. They must be open to feedback and willing to continuously improve their skills and knowledge.

● Adaptability: Since teams organize themselves and tasks often vary, team members must be flexible and adaptable. They should be able to react quickly to changes and be ready to take on new challenges.

Training procedure

Implementing the Spotify model requires thorough training of team members. Here are some strategies that have proven effective:

● Workshops: Workshops are a great way to teach the basics of the Spotify model and provide hands-on training. They can be led by internal or external experts and should cover the basic principles and practices of the model.

- Mentoring and coaching: Mentoring and coaching can help support team members on an individual level. A mentor or coach can help develop individual skills and knowledge, overcome challenges, and deepen understanding of the Spotify model.

- Self-directed learning: It can also be helpful to provide team members with resources for self-directed learning, such as online courses, books, or articles. This way, they can develop their knowledge and skills at their own pace.

- Learning by doing: The best way to learn is often by simply starting and learning from practice. By working directly in squads, team members can see the Spotify model in action and hone their skills over time.

The selection and training of team members is a critical factor in the success of the Spotify model. By carefully selecting team members who embody the core principles of the model and providing effective training programs, an organization can take full advantage of this innovative approach.

Identify the necessary skills and attributes for team members

Selecting the right team members is a critical factor in the success of the Spotify model. This is because at the heart of this model is the principle of autonomous teams, in which each member understands his or her role and responsibilities and proactively contributes to the achievement of common goals. Therefore, it is crucial to identify the key skills and attributes that each member of such a team should possess. Let's look at some of these key skills and attributes.

SPOTIFY MODEL: PRACTICAL IMPLEMENTATION GUIDE

Skills

Technical expertise: Technical expertise requirements may vary depending on the nature of the task and the project. However, it is important that each team member has solid knowledge and skills in their area of expertise to contribute to the team's goal achievement.

Project management: Since teams work autonomously under the Spotify model, members must have basic project management skills. These include the ability to prioritize tasks, use resources effectively, and monitor project progress.

Communication and collaboration: The ability to communicate and collaborate effectively is essential. This includes both verbal and written communication, as well as the ability to give and receive feedback constructively.

Features

Personal responsibility: The members of autonomous teams must take responsibility for their own tasks. This requires a high degree of personal responsibility and self-motivation.

Adaptability: In a dynamic work environment such as the Spotify model, team members must be flexible and adaptable. They must be ready to adapt to changing priorities and tasks and to take on new challenges.

Team orientation: A fundamental feature of the Spotify model is team collaboration. Therefore, team members should be team-oriented and always keep the well-being of the entire team in mind.

Willingness to learn: Continuous improvement and development is a key aspect of the Spotify model. Therefore, team members must be willing to learn and constantly strive to expand their skills and knowledge.

By identifying these key skills and attributes, you can ensure that you select the right people for your team and deploy them according to their strengths and capabilities. This way, you can realize your team's full potential and ensure a smooth transition to the Spotify model.

Introduction to training procedures and programs for the Spotify model.

To ease the transition to a new way of working, like the Spotify model, training programs are essential. They serve to build employees' knowledge and skills, help them understand the new work environment and culture, and give them the tools and resources they need to be successful. The following are some training practices and programs that can be helpful in implementing the Spotify model.

- Onboarding Training: When introducing new employees to the Spotify model, onboarding training sessions are critical. They should include an introduction to the Spotify model, an explanation of its key elements and expected ways of working, and specific information about the employee's role and responsibilities on the team.

- Workshops and seminars: These can be used to reinforce specific aspects of the Spotify model, such as the role of Squads, Tribes, Chapters, and Guilds, or prioritization and project management methods. Such events can also be a good opportunity to share best practices and learn from the experiences of others.

● E-learning courses: Digital learning platforms can be a flexible and efficient way to provide the necessary training. They can be tailored to the individual needs of employees and offer the opportunity to integrate learning into daily working life.

● Mentoring and coaching: Individual mentoring can be particularly helpful in helping employees adapt to the Spotify model. Experienced employees or external consultants can act as mentors or coaches and provide valuable insight and advice.

● Practical exercises: Nothing can replace direct experience. Therefore, exercises, simulations and projects that apply the principles and practices of the Spotify model can help employees internalize what they have learned and understand the new way of working.

These training procedures and programs represent just a few ways you can prepare your employees for the transition to the Spotify model. The better trained and prepared your employees are, the smoother the transition will be and the more successful your company will be in implementing the new model.

Case studies and examples for selection and training of team members

To illustrate the importance and effectiveness of well-designed selection processes and training programs, let's look at some real-world examples.

Case study 1: ABC Bank

When ABC Bank decided to implement the Spotify model, they knew that the key to success was selecting the right employees and providing effective training. The bank placed a strong focus on recruiting employees with a strong "willingness to learn" and the ability to quickly adapt to changing environments. They relied on a mix of onboarding training, workshops, and e-learning to give their employees the knowledge and skills they needed. This approach paid off and ABC was able to successfully implement the Spotify model into their operations.

Case study 2: BDQ Media

BDQ Media, a digital media company, had a different approach to introducing the Spotify model. They hired "Agile Coaches" to train their employees and guide them through the transition to the new working model. These coaches played a critical role in training employees, helping to implement the new ways of working, and being a key link between the different teams and departments. This special kind of support enabled BDQ Media to successfully master the transition and establish an effective, agile way of working.

Case study 3: ZT Bank

ZT Bank, a UK mobile bank, focused on training their employees through real-world experience. They used "squads" as a core element of their learning approach, with new employees joining existing squads and being coached by more experienced colleagues. In this way, new employees were able to learn the principles and methods of the Spotify model first-hand and put them directly into practice.

These examples show that it is not only a matter of selecting the right people, but also the way in which they are trained. The training strategy must be tailored to the specific company, its culture and its employees. With the right selection and training of team members, a company can effectively implement the Spotify model and reap its full benefits.

3.5 Setting realistic goals and adjusting expectations over time

Transforming a company according to the Spotify model is a complex process that requires time, effort and resources. It is therefore critical to set realistic goals and adjust expectations over time. This section focuses on how this can be achieved.

Setting realistic goals

Realistic goals are the backbone of any successful business transformation. The transition to the Spotify model is about creating a culture of continuous improvement, learning and adaptation, and this cannot be achieved overnight. It requires patience and perseverance.

At the start of the transition, goals should be both achievable and measurable. Instead of abstract goals such as "better collaboration," they should include quantifiable results, e.g., "a 20% reduction in interdependencies between teams." It is important to consider both short-term and long-term goals. Short-term goals can help maintain employee engagement and motivation, while long-term goals set the direction and overall goal of the transformation.

Adjustment of expectations over time

The transition to the Spotify model is a dynamic process. Certain assumptions or expectations made at the beginning of the transformation may need to be adjusted over time. This may be required due to unforeseen challenges, changes in business strategy, or employee feedback and learning experiences.

It is important not to view these changes as failures, but as part of the learning and adaptation process. Open communication, regular feedback and transparency are key elements to ensure that all team members are aware of and support the changes.

Over time, the company will also get a better idea of what works and what doesn't in the context of the Spotify model. This knowledge should be used to continuously adjust expectations and refine the implementation.

Case studies: Realistic goals and adjustment of expectations

A good example of this is the software company HubSpot. When it decided to adopt the Spotify model, it started by setting realistic goals for the first phase of the transition. It placed a particular focus on preparing its teams to work and make decisions more independently. Over time, the company adjusted its expectations and goals based on feedback from its employees and lessons learned during implementation.

Another example is ABC. The company started its transition to the Spotify model with clear, measurable goals. It placed a strong focus on optimizing its processes and improving the work environment. Over time, however, it adjusted its expectations, recognizing that some goals and methods were not optimal in their original form.

In summary, setting realistic goals and adjusting expectations over time are essential components of implementing the Spotify model. It is an ongoing process that requires flexibility, learning and adaptation. By addressing these aspects, companies can effectively integrate the Spotify model into their organization and benefit from it.

How to set realistic goals for moving to the Spotify model

Transitioning to an agile way of working based on the Spotify model is a journey that requires a clear vision, careful planning, and defined goals. This section covers the various aspects that need to be considered in order to set realistic goals for the transition.

Clarity about the "why

Before setting out to set specific goals, it is important to understand the "why" behind the change. What are the key drivers for change? What benefits does one hope to gain from implementing the Spotify model? The answers to these questions provide the guidelines for setting goals.

SMART principle

Setting goals according to the SMART principle is a proven method that is also used in the context of the Spotify model. SMART stands for Specific, Measurable, Achievable, Relevant, and Time-bound.

- Specific: Goals should be clear and precise. Instead of a general goal such as "improve team performance", a more specific goal should be set, e.g. "increase the number of successfully completed projects per team and quarter".

- Measurable: Each goal should be measurable to assess progress and determine when the goal is achieved.

- Achievable: Goals must be realistic and achievable. An overly ambitious goal can cause employees to feel overwhelmed and lose motivation.

- Relevant: Goals should be relevant to the business objectives and vision of the transformation.

- Time-bound: A clear time frame creates a sense of urgency and helps maintain focus.

Short-term and long-term goals

It is helpful to set both short-term and long-term goals. Short-term goals provide milestones that make progress visible and encourage motivation. Long-term goals, on the other hand, provide direction and keep the big picture in view.

For example, a short-term goal could be to form the first squads and make them functional within three months. A long-term goal, on the other hand, could be to achieve a complete agile transformation within two years.

Involvement of employees

It is also important to involve employees in the goal-setting process. They can offer valuable insight into feasible goals, and their involvement increases engagement and acceptance.

Setting realistic goals is a critical step in the planning phase of the transition to the Spotify model. By considering the above aspects, companies can define goals that pave the way for a successful agile transformation.

Adjustment of goals and expectations based on progress and feedback

One of the basic principles of agile working and thus also of the Spotify model is the ability to adapt and change. This very principle also applies to goal setting during the transformation process. This section explains how goals and expectations can be adjusted based on progress and feedback.

Iterative goal setting

The Spotify model emphasizes the importance of iterations and continuous improvement. These agile principles can also be applied to goal setting. Instead of rigidly pursuing goals once they have been set, progress should be regularly evaluated and goals adjusted accordingly. This iterative approach enables rapid response to change and improves the company's ability to focus on realistic and achievable goals.

Feedback as the key to adaptation

An effective way to assess progress and adjust goals is to systematically solicit and use feedback. This can take the form of regular feedback sessions, surveys, or informal conversations. Feedback should come from everyone involved, including squad members, product owners, Agile coaches, and stakeholders.

Using feedback to adjust goals has several advantages. It makes it possible to identify problems early on and take corrective action. In addition, feedback can help to involve employees more in the transformation process and promote their commitment.

Dealing with unfulfilled expectations

The changeover process does not always go as originally planned. Obstacles may arise, unforeseen difficulties may arise, or the intended benefits may not materialize as quickly as hoped. In such cases, it is important to react flexibly to these challenges and adjust goals and expectations accordingly.

It is also critical to communicate openly about these challenges and foster an understanding that change takes time and setbacks are part of the process. In this way, employee engagement can be maintained and a culture of continuous improvement fostered.

Conclusion

Aligning goals and expectations is a key aspect of agile working and the Spotify model. Regularly reviewing progress, soliciting feedback, and being flexible in dealing with challenges can effectively manage the transition to the Spotify model and ensure the success of the transformation process.

***

Examples of goal setting and alignment of expectations in organizations that have implemented the Spotify model include

Real-world experience can shed vivid light on theory and facilitate the implementation of concepts. The following are two examples of goal setting and alignment of expectations in companies that have successfully implemented the Spotify model.

Company A: Start with small steps and regular review

Company A, a mid-sized software developer, decided to implement the Spotify model to improve the agility and efficiency of their development processes. They initially set a clear goal: to transition from two traditional development teams to squads within one quarter.

The company took a step-by-step approach to this change. They set up regular feedback sessions to monitor progress and involve employees in the change process. In the process, they found that the transition was taking more time than expected. However, instead of sticking to the original schedule, they adjusted their goals and extended the transition period.

By taking feedback into account and adjusting their goals, the company was able to successfully manage the transition. While the process took longer than originally planned, the quality of the transition and employee engagement were higher.

Company B: Dealing with unfulfilled expectations

Company B, a large telecommunications company, started its transformation with high expectations. Their goal was to cut the time-to-market for new products in half. They believed that the Spotify model could help them achieve this ambitious goal.

Despite the successful implementation of the model, after one year the company found that time-to-market had improved only slightly. Instead of considering the change a failure, they used this feedback to adjust their expectations and conduct a detailed analysis.

They found that other factors outside their agile teams were affecting time-to-market. As a result, they adjusted their strategy and began to improve these areas as well. As a result, Company B was able to benefit from adopting the Spotify model despite initial difficulties and unmet expectations.

These examples demonstrate the importance of being flexible and adaptable when it comes to goal setting and adjusting expectations during the implementation of the Spotify model. By considering progress and feedback, and being willing to adapt, organizations can effectively manage the transition and ensure long-term success.

Practical examples and case studies for the implementation of the model

To gain a more comprehensive understanding of how the Spotify model is applied in the real world, it is helpful to look at some real-world examples and case studies. In this section, we present three in-depth case studies that highlight various aspects and challenges of implementing the Spotify model. The case studies are from companies of different sizes and from different industries to illustrate the breadth of possible applications of this model.

Case study 1: Company C - A large company in the technology sector

Company C is a leading provider of cloud services and has several thousand employees. Despite its size, the company strives to remain agile and bring innovative solutions to market quickly. To achieve these goals, it decided to implement the Spotify model.

The transition began with the formation of small squads and tribes within specific business units. Over time, the model was extended to the entire company. The transition was a significant challenge, as it required a significant culture change.

During the transition, Company C realized that adopting the Spotify model was not just a structural change, but more importantly a change in corporate culture. They learned that it is important to focus on people and to encourage their autonomy and creativity.

Case study 2: Company D - A start-up in the financial sector

Company D is an emerging fintech startup. From the beginning, their goal was to create an agile and flexible work environment that encourages innovation. That's why they chose the Spotify model.

The challenges they faced were different than those of a large company. With a small team, they had to find ways to effectively manage roles within squads and communication between squads. They found that holding regular "Guild" meetings and establishing a strong feedback culture were critical to success.

Case study 3: Company E - A medium-sized manufacturing company

Company E is a traditional manufacturing company that decided to become more agile to respond to rapidly changing market demands. They implemented the Spotify model in their IT department.

One of the biggest challenges for Company E was to foster understanding and acceptance of the Spotify model and agile ways of working in general in an otherwise traditionally run company.

However, through training, workshops and ongoing communication, they were able to create a deeper understanding of the model and demonstrate the benefits to the business. They were able to gain strong support at both management and employee levels, which was critical to the successful transition.

These case studies illustrate that implementing the Spotify model presents both challenges and opportunities, and that each organization must find its own path to agility. However, it is clear that strong leadership, open communication, and a focus on employees are critical to a successful transition.

Detailed description of the implementation of the Spotify model in different organizations.

To fully grasp the potential and applicability of the Spotify model, we now look at the implementation processes in three organizations that differ in size, scope of work, and prior organizational structure.

Organization A - A global software company

Organization A, a renowned software company, faced the challenge of remaining agile and adapting quickly to market changes despite its size. To achieve this, it decided to implement the Spotify model.

The first phase of the transition focused on the formation of small, cross-functional teams - "squads." Each squad was made responsible for a specific aspect of the overall product.

The Squads were then grouped into larger "Tribes" based on the commonality of their product functions. The formation of these Tribes allowed for effective communication and collaboration between Squads.

Implementation of the Spotify model was an ongoing process at Organization A, supported by regular "retrospectives" and continuous improvement. In the retrospectives, each squad analyzed its performance and identified areas for improvement.

Organization B - A young technology start-up

Organization B, a technology startup, adopted the Spotify model from the beginning. With a small team of about 30 people, they divided into several squads, with each squad working on a specific product feature.

The challenges at Organization B were different from those at Organization A. With fewer resources, they had to find innovative ways to maximize productivity and optimize communication between squads. Guilds and chapters helped by providing opportunities for knowledge sharing and collaboration between squads.

Organization C - A traditional insurance company

Organization C, an insurance company with several hundred employees, was looking for ways to become more agile and drive innovation. They decided on the Spotify model and started implementing it in their IT department.

In Organization C, the challenge lay in the need to change the existing corporate culture and make employees more aware of the benefits of the Spotify model. However, with the help of workshops, training programs and continuous communication, the company was able to gradually bring about changes in its organizational structure and culture.

These three examples show how the Spotify model has been implemented in different contexts. They also illustrate the challenges and benefits that can come with implementing this model. It is clear that the Spotify model must be adapted to the specific needs of each organization in order to be effective.

Challenges, successes and lessons learned from these examples

With the case studies presented, we have gained an initial insight into the practical application of the Spotify model. In the following, we analyze the experiences of these companies by highlighting the challenges they overcame, the successes they achieved, and the lessons they learned from the process.

Organization A - A global software company

Organization A's challenge was to promote agility in a large, well-established company. Their key successes included creating small, agile teams that were able to respond quickly to market changes. The most valuable lesson they learned was that change takes time and is an ongoing process that needs constant review and adjustment.

Organization B - A young technology start-up

As a start-up, Organization B was faced with the challenge of maximizing productivity with limited resources. Despite this challenge, the company was able to successfully launch several product features in a timely manner. They learned that it was important to have flexible communication channels that fostered knowledge sharing and collaboration between squads.

Organization C - A traditional insurance company

Organization C's biggest challenge was changing their existing culture. They were able to successfully foster innovation and agility in their organization. The most important lesson they learned from the process was that employees are the backbone of any change and their involvement and support are critical to success.

Despite the different contexts and challenges, all three organizations had similar experiences. The Spotify model enabled them to be agile and adaptable while fostering team cohesion and productivity. However, it has become equally clear that implementing the Spotify model is not off-the-shelf, but requires a conscious effort tailored to the specific organization. It is a process that requires patience, continuous adjustments, and commitment from all team members.

Guidance on how to apply these insights in your own business

The case studies and their analysis so far offer us many valuable insights. But how can you apply them to your own business? Below are some steps and considerations that can help you implement the Spotify model.

1. analysis of your current situation

First, you should analyze your current operational status. How are your teams structured? How does communication flow? What is working well and what could be improved? You should use both qualitative and quantitative data in this analysis. Interview your employees, conduct surveys, and analyze performance data.

2. define your goals

Before you start implementing the Spotify model, it is important to clearly define what you want to achieve. Do you want to improve agility? Boost communication? Accelerate the innovation process? Make sure these goals are SMART (Specific, Measurable, Achievable, Realistic, Time-bound) and understood by all stakeholders.

3. develop an implementation plan

Once you have defined your goals, you should create a detailed implementation plan. This plan should include the steps to implement the Spotify model, the roles and responsibilities of team members, and the expected challenges and possible solutions.

4. create a supportive culture

Implementing the Spotify model requires a corporate culture that welcomes and supports change. Foster a culture of openness and respect, where everyone has the right to express their opinion and propose new ideas. Encourage your employees to continuously learn and develop.

5. check and adjust

Implementing the Spotify model is an ongoing process. It is important to regularly review whether you are achieving your goals and whether the process is effective. Based on these reviews, you should be ready to make adjustments and change your approach accordingly.

Remember that implementing the Spotify model is not a quick fix, but a long-term investment that requires patience and commitment. Use the lessons and experiences from the case studies presented to make this process as smooth and effective as possible.

Part 4: Measure success and make adjustments

4.1 Selection and definition of metrics

To measure and monitor the success of your implementation of the Spotify model, it is critical to define clear and measurable metrics. Metrics are standardized measurements used to quantify progress, performance, and quality. Choosing the right metrics is critical because they help guide focus, make informed decisions, and drive continuous improvement. But how do you choose the right metrics and how do you define them? Here are some important points to consider.

Relevance of the metrics

The metrics you choose should be directly relevant to your specific goals and context. It doesn't make sense to measure something that doesn't have a direct impact on your team's performance or the achievement of your goals. For example, if you want to improve your team's productivity, you should select metrics that measure workload, project timelines, or the number of tasks completed.

SMART Metrics

The metrics you select should be SMART - meaning they should be Specific, Measurable, Attainable, Realistic, and Time-bound. Specific means the metric should be clearly defined and easy to understand. Measurable means that the metric can be quantified and tracked. Attainable means that the goals associated with the metric can be achieved with reasonable effort. Realistic means that the metric is appropriate within the context and resources of your organization. Time-bound means that the metric should be measured and reviewed within a specific time frame.

Balance between quantitative and qualitative metrics

Although quantitative metrics - those that can be measured in numbers - are often easier to track and compare, they should not be the only type of metrics you use. Qualitative metrics, such as employee feedback or customer satisfaction, can also provide valuable insights and should also be considered.

Avoidance of vanity metrics

Vanity metrics are numbers that look good but have no real meaning. They can be easily manipulated and often do not provide real insight into performance. For example, the number of employees in a company may be considered a vanity metric if it does not correlate with productivity or efficiency. It is important to avoid these types of metrics and instead focus on those that provide real value.

Metrics review and adjustment

Finally, you should regularly review and adjust your metrics. What was relevant at the beginning of implementing the Spotify model may not be a year later. Check regularly to see if your metrics are still relevant and if they are helping you achieve your goals.

By carefully selecting and defining metrics, you can effectively measure and monitor the success of your implementation of the Spotify model. This enables you to make informed decisions and continuously improve your processes.

Overview of possible metrics for measuring the success of the Spotify model

Metrics are critical to measuring the success of the Spotify model. They provide quantifiable data that serves as a reference point for improving processes and identifying problem areas. Here's an overview of some metrics that may prove useful as you implement the Spotify model in your organization.

1. delivery speed

Delivery velocity is a quantitative metric that measures the speed at which your team completes work orders. It is typically measured as the number of units of work completed in a given time period. This metric can tell you how efficient your team is and whether improvements are needed.

2. cycle time

Cycle time measures the time it takes to process a task or work order from start to completion. A low cycle time is often an indicator of high efficiency and productivity. It can also help identify bottlenecks in your processes.

3. employee satisfaction

Employee satisfaction is a qualitative metric that is often captured through regular surveys or feedback sessions. It can tell you how your employees feel about their work environment and whether they feel connected to the company's values and goals. High employee satisfaction can lead to higher productivity and lower turnover rates.

4. number of innovations

The number of innovations is a qualitative metric that measures the number of new ideas or improvements proposed by your team during a given period. This metric can be an indicator of how creative and engaged your team is.

5. customer satisfaction

Customer satisfaction is another important qualitative metric that can be measured through customer feedback, surveys or reviews. It provides insight into how well your team is meeting customers' needs and expectations.

6. error rate

Error rate is a quantitative metric that measures how many errors or problems occurred during a specific time period. A high error rate may indicate problems in your processes and should be addressed for improvement.

These metrics are just a few of the many you can use to measure the success of your implementation of the Spotify model. It's important to remember that your choice of metrics should depend on your organization's specific goals and context.

How to define metrics that best reflect the success of the model

Defining metrics that best reflect the success of the Spotify model is essential to a successful implementation. Here are some steps to help you determine these key performance metrics:

1. determine your goals

First, you should clearly define what you want to achieve by implementing the Spotify model. These goals could include, for example, higher productivity, more innovation, or better employee satisfaction. Your goals will serve as the basis for selecting the metrics to measure.

2. select relevant metrics

Next, you should select metrics that are directly related to your goals. For example, if your goal is higher productivity, you could use metrics like delivery speed or cycle time. If your goal is more innovation, you could measure the number of new ideas proposed by your team.

3. define clear benchmarks

For each metric you select, you should define clear benchmarks. For example, a metric could be that your team should complete a certain number of units of work or propose a certain number of new ideas within a certain period of time.

4. monitor and analyze your metrics

Once you have defined your metrics and benchmarks, you should monitor and analyze them regularly. This will help you track your team's progress and see if you are achieving your goals.

5. adjust your metrics as needed

It is important to remember that defining metrics is not a one-time event. You should be prepared to adjust your metrics as needed, especially if you find that they are not providing the information you want or if your goals change.

In summary, selecting and defining metrics is a critical process in implementing the Spotify model. By setting clear goals, selecting relevant metrics, defining clear benchmarks, and regularly monitoring and analyzing your metrics, you can ensure that you are effectively measuring and managing your team's success.

Case studies and examples of the successful application of metrics

The successful application of metrics is an essential part of implementing the Spotify model. By assessing progress against measurable metrics, organizations can objectively evaluate the success of their efforts. Here are some examples and case studies that illustrate this:

Case study 1: The technology company ABC

ABC is a technology company that chose the Spotify model to make its software development teams more effective. The company set three main goals: increase productivity, improve quality, and increase employee satisfaction.

To measure productivity, ABC used the metric of "speed of delivery," defined as the number of units of work a team completes within a given time period. To measure quality, ABC monitored the number of post-release errors. And to measure employee satisfaction, ABC conducted regular surveys of employees.

By monitoring these metrics, ABC saw that productivity and quality improved after implementing the Spotify model. Employee satisfaction also increased, as evidenced by positive survey results and lower turnover rates.

Case study 2: The XYZ retail chain

XYZ is a retail chain that adopted the Spotify model to improve its internal processes and drive innovation. Their main goals were to increase efficiency and to increase the number of new ideas.

To measure efficiency, XYZ monitored cycle time, the time from the start of a project to its completion. To measure innovation, XYZ counted the number of new ideas proposed by employees.

By regularly reviewing these metrics, XYZ was able to see that efficiency improved after implementing the Spotify model, and they also noticed a significant increase in the number of new ideas proposed.

These examples show how the right selection and application of metrics can help organizations evaluate the success of their implementation of the Spotify model and achieve their goals. Every organization is unique, and choosing the right metrics depends on the organization's specific goals and challenges. But as these case studies show, the right use of metrics can go a long way toward achieving those goals.

4.2 Monitoring progress

Implementing the Spotify model in your organization is an ongoing process, and continuously monitoring its progress is critical to its success. It allows you to determine if your efforts are going in the right direction and which areas may need further adjustments. But how exactly do you effectively monitor progress? In this section, we'll look at some techniques and approaches that can help you do that.

Use of dashboards

A common way to monitor the progress of your Spotify model implementation is to use dashboards. A dashboard is a visual tool that gives you an overview of your project's key metrics and indicators. It can help you spot trends, identify performance issues, and make informed decisions.

In a dashboard for the Spotify model, you could display metrics such as delivery speed, defect rate, employee satisfaction, and many others. By comparing these metrics over time, you can see if you're making progress and if certain teams or areas need special attention.

Regular reviews and feedback loops

Another important aspect of monitoring progress is regular reviews and feedback loops. In the Spotify model, this is achieved through so-called "retrospectives". A retrospective is a meeting held at the end of each sprint or cycle where the team reviews its work and process.

During a retrospective, the team reflects on what went well and what could be improved. They also use this opportunity to give and receive feedback. These regular reviews and feedback loops allow you to continuously learn and improve, and are an important part of monitoring your progress.

Use of project management tools

Project management tools can also be a valuable aid in monitoring your progress. Tools like Jira, Trello, Asana, and others can help you organize your work, track progress, and ensure you stay on track.

These tools allow you to record your tasks and goals, monitor the progress of tasks and projects, and they often provide reporting features that allow you to visualize and analyze your progress.

Involvement of all stakeholders

Finally, when monitoring progress, it is important to involve all stakeholders. This means that not only management, but also team members and other stakeholders should receive regular updates on progress.

This can be achieved through regular meetings, reports and updates. It is important that this communication is open and honest and that it highlights both successes and challenges. This way, everyone in the company can understand and contribute to progress.

Overall, monitoring progress is a critical aspect of implementing the Spotify model. By using dashboards, regular reviews and feedback loops, project management tools, and engaging all stakeholders, you can ensure that you are on track and that your efforts are going in the desired direction.

Methods and tools for monitoring the progress of the transition to the Spotify model

Transitioning to a new way of working, such as the Spotify model, is a challenge that requires diligent monitoring and fine-tuning. To monitor the progress and effectiveness of this transition, there are a variety of methods and tools that we will discuss in more detail in this section.

Agile metrics

Agile metrics are essential to the monitoring process. They provide quantifiable data that can be used to evaluate the progress and performance of your transition to the Spotify model. Some common Agile metrics are delivery speed, cycle time, and defect rate.

Delivery velocity is a metric that shows how many units of work (e.g., user stories or tasks) a team completes within a sprint or cycle. It can help evaluate the productivity and efficiency of the team.

Cycle time measures the length of time it takes a unit of work to go from start to completion. A short cycle time usually indicates high efficiency.

The defect rate is a measure of the quality of work. It measures the ratio of defective work units to the total number of completed work units. A low defect rate indicates high quality work.

Project Management Software

Project management software can be a powerful tool for monitoring progress. It allows tracking tasks, visualizing progress and organizing workflow. Some of the most popular software tools in this area are Jira, Asana and Trello.

Jira is a versatile tool that is great for Agile teams. It allows you to create, assign, and track tasks, and it offers extensive reporting capabilities.

Asana is another powerful tool that is appreciated for its user-friendly interface and its ability to collaborate easily. It allows tracking tasks, projects and milestones in a simple way.

Trello, known for its Kanban boards, is another great tool for visualizing progress and organizing work.

Retrospectives

Retrospectives are a method from the agile work environment used to regularly review the team's progress and performance. They are usually scheduled at the end of a sprint or cycle and provide an opportunity for the team to look back on their work, celebrate successes, and identify areas for improvement.

A retrospective often follows a specific format: "What went well," "What didn't go well," and "What we will do differently in the next iteration." This encourages open and constructive discussion and helps the team to continuously learn and improve.

Stakeholder engagement

Another important aspect of monitoring progress is stakeholder engagement. This includes regular updates, meetings, and reports to ensure that all stakeholders are aware of the status of the transition and can provide input.

In summary, a combination of agile metrics, project management software, retrospectives, and stakeholder engagement are the most effective methods and tools for monitoring progress as you transition to the Spotify model. They allow you to keep a close eye on the process and make the necessary adjustments to ensure your transition is successful.

How to create and interpret progress reports

Continuation reports are an important part of any successful business transformation. They provide a clear representation of current status, highlight performance trends, and identify areas that need improvement. Here is a guide to creating and interpreting progress reports in the context of the transition to the Spotify model.

Preparation of progress reports

First, you need to decide what information to include in your report. This can vary, but should at least cover the following points:

1. Status of scheduled tasks: An overview of the tasks that have been completed within the defined timeframe, as well as those that are still outstanding. This shows if the team is on track or if adjustments are needed.
2. Agile Metrics: As mentioned earlier, metrics such as delivery speed, cycle time, and defect rate can provide valuable insights into team performance and efficiency.
3. Challenges and obstacles: Each report should also highlight difficulties or challenges that the team encountered during the transition process. This can range from technical difficulties to cultural resistance.
4. Successes and Achievements: It is important to highlight and celebrate successes to motivate the team and recognize progress.
5. Next Steps: Finally, the report should identify the next planned steps or goals for the upcoming period.

The presentation of this information may vary. You can use a combination of text, charts, graphs, or tables to present the data in an appealing and easy-to-understand way.

Interpretation of progress reports

The interpretation of a progress report is as important as its preparation. It is used to turn the report into usable findings and actions. Here are some points that can help you with interpretation:

1. Evaluate productivity: Look at delivery speed and cycle time. Are they consistent, improving or deteriorating? This can help you evaluate the efficiency of the team.
2. Analyze the quality: Look at the error rate. Is it low or is it increasing? A high defect rate could indicate quality issues that need to be addressed.
3. Identify problems and challenges: What barriers are mentioned in the report? How do they affect the transition process? What actions are being taken to overcome them?
4. Identify successes: What successes have been achieved? How have they contributed to the progress of the transition process?
5. Plan the next steps: What are the planned next steps? Are they realistic and in line with progress to date?

Creating and interpreting progress reports on a regular basis allows you to continuously monitor, manage, and optimize the transition process to the Spotify model. It is a critical tool to ensure that the transition is successful and delivers the desired results.

Case studies and examples of effective monitoring of progress

In this section, we take a look at some specific examples of how companies have been able to monitor the progress of their transition to the Spotify model.

Case study 1: Technology start-up "TechAce

"TechAce is a growing technology startup that decided to adopt the Spotify model to make their development team more agile. They relied on weekly sprint reviews and quarterly reviews to monitor progress. The sprint reviews reviewed individual tasks and short-term goals, while the quarterly reviews analyzed the team's long-term goals and overall direction.

They also created a central dashboard to visualize agile metrics, including cycle time, delivery speed, and defect rate. This dashboard was updated regularly and was accessible to all team members. It was considered an effective tool for increasing visibility and identifying areas for improvement.

Case study 2: Large company "CorpMax

"CorpMax", a global company with multiple teams and locations, had a major challenge implementing the Spotify model. To keep track of progress, "CorpMax" relied on a combination of regular reports and technical tools.

They relied on monthly progress reports created by each team and shared with managers. These reports included details on tasks completed, obstacles the team had encountered, and next steps planned.

In addition, "CorpMax" introduced project management software that provided a real-time overview of the progress of the various teams. This software allowed management to track the progress of the teams and intervene quickly when necessary.

Case study 3: Medium-sized software company "SASrV

"SASrV", a mid-sized software company, already had a strong culture of collaboration and transparency before adopting the Spotify model. They used this to their advantage by introducing regular town hall meetings where progress reports were shared with all employees.

In addition to the town hall meetings, "SASrV" also used agile project management tool to monitor progress. This tool provided a visual board that showed the status of various tasks and provided reports that showed the team's performance over time.

These case studies show that there are many ways to monitor progress in implementing the Spotify model. Depending on the size, culture, and needs of the organization, different approaches and tools can be combined to ensure effective monitoring. It turns out that a combination of regular reports, visual dashboards, and collaboration tools often yields the best results.

———————

4.3 Evaluation of the results

Effective implementation of the Spotify model requires not only careful planning and execution, but also thorough evaluation of results. The process of evaluation enables organizations to recognize the impact of their efforts, celebrate successes, and identify potential areas for improvement. However, evaluating results is not a simple process. It requires a strategic approach and a thorough understanding of the metrics and indicators that best reflect success.

First, it is important that companies understand that the results of implementing the Spotify model cannot be expressed only in quantitative measures. While metrics such as productivity, cycle time and delivery speed are important indicators of success, there are also qualitative aspects that should be considered. These include factors such as employee satisfaction, team dynamics and culture change, which are equally important to assess the overall success of the implementation.

Evaluation should take place at several levels. At the individual level, performance evaluations and feedback sessions can reveal how well individual employees have adapted to the new model. At the team level, retrospectives and team meetings can be used to assess interaction within the team and identify areas for improvement. At the company level, a comprehensive review of business goals and performance indicators can reveal whether the Spotify model has helped improve the company's overall performance.

There are several methods to conduct these assessments. Surveys and questionnaires can be used to collect feedback from employees and measure employee satisfaction. Analytical tools can be used to collect and analyze data to provide an overview of organizational performance. Interviews and focus groups can provide deeper insights into employee experiences and perceptions.

The results of these assessments should not be considered in isolation. Instead, they should be embedded in a larger context and considered in the context of the goals and expectations set. Only in this way can a clear picture of the success of the implementation of the Spotify model be achieved.

Finally, the evaluation of results should not be a one-time event. It should be a continuous process that is repeated at regular intervals. This allows companies to track changes and trends over time and adjust their strategies accordingly.

In summary, outcomes assessment is a critical part of the process of implementing the Spotify model. It allows companies to measure the success of their efforts and understand how they can further improve their practices to achieve their goals. By taking a structured and strategic approach to evaluation, organizations can ensure they are getting the best results from their implementation of the Spotify model.

Evaluating the Implementation of the Spotify Model: A Practice Guide

A proper evaluation of the implementation of the Spotify model will allow you to measure the success of your efforts and identify areas for improvement. However, it is not always easy to quantify and qualify the value and impact of such a significant organizational change. Below are some steps and guidelines that can help you effectively assess results.

1. determination of the evaluation criteria:

Before you begin your evaluation, it's important to define what success means to your business. What goals were you trying to achieve by implementing the Spotify model? Did you want to increase the speed of product development? Did you want to achieve greater alignment with customer needs? Or was your goal to foster a stronger culture of collaboration and ownership? These goals should serve as guidelines for your evaluation.

2. collection and analysis of data:

The assessment should be based on solid data. This can be a combination of quantitative data (such as productivity metrics, cycle times, etc.) and qualitative data (such as employee feedback, team dynamics, etc.). Project management and software metrics analysis tools, surveys, and interviews can help with data collection.

3. contextual analysis:

Data alone does not provide a complete picture. It must be put in the context of your business and your specific goals and challenges. For example, an increase in productivity may be a good sign, but if it is accompanied by a decrease in employee satisfaction, it may indicate long-term problems.

4. continuous evaluation:

Evaluating the implementation of the Spotify model should not be a one-time event, but an ongoing process. You should create regular progress reports and monitor results. This way, you can identify trends, track performance over time, and adjust your strategies accordingly.

5. learning and adapting:

Finally, evaluation should be used not only to measure results, but also to learn from them. Use the results to improve your practices, make changes, and further refine your model.

Evaluating the implementation of the Spotify model can be a challenging task, but it is a critical step on the path to a successful agile transformation. With a clear understanding of your goals, solid data, and a continuous improvement process, you can realize the full value of your implementation.

Make changes and adjust plans based on evaluation results

Implementing the Spotify model in your organization is not a static process. It requires continuous monitoring, adjustment, and optimization to achieve maximum value. Here are some tips on how to make changes and adjust your plans based on the assessment results.

1. understand the results:

The first step is to fully understand the results of your assessment. What does the data tell you? How do you interpret the results in the context of your business goals and needs? What patterns or trends are apparent? Take the time to thoroughly analyze and interpret the data.

2. Identify successes and challenges:

Divide the results into two categories: What worked well and what presented challenges? The successes will give you insight into the strengths of your approach, while the challenges will highlight areas that need improvement.

3. develop improvement plans:

For each identified area of challenge, you should develop an improvement plan. This could include adjusting your processes, training your people, changing your tools, or adjusting your organizational structure.

4. implement changes:

Once you have developed your improvement plans, implement them. This can be done in stages to minimize the impact on operations and reduce the risk of disruption. Remember to inform your employees about the changes and explain to them why these changes are necessary.

5. monitor the effects:

After implementing the changes, monitor the impact. This should be done again by collecting and analyzing data. Pay particular attention to the areas where you have targeted improvements.

6. adjust and repeat:

Then adjust your plans and approaches based on the latest results. This is a continuous cycle of learning and improving.

Implementing the Spotify model is a dynamic journey, and the ability to adapt and learn based on results is a critical factor for success. With a systematic approach to evaluation and improvement, you can ensure your organization is getting the most out of the model.

————————

Case studies and examples for the evaluation of results and resulting changes

Case study 1: AlphaTech software development company

AlphaTech is a mid-sized software development company that specializes in developing custom business solutions. It began its journey to implement the Spotify model with the hope of improving the efficiency of its software development and fostering a stronger corporate culture of collaboration.

After a year of implementation, AlphaTech conducted a comprehensive review. The results showed improved efficiency and employee satisfaction, but there were also challenges, such as a lack of communication between some squads and tribes and a decline in code quality in some projects.

Based on these findings, AlphaTech implemented several changes. It initiated a series of cross-tribe meetings to improve communication and used code reviews to ensure code quality. One year after these changes, AlphaTech reported better communication between teams and improved code quality.

Case study 2: Global e-commerce giant EcomWorld

EcomWorld is a leading e-commerce company with thousands of employees. It implemented the Spotify model to improve the way it handles the complexity of its global operations.

After implementation and a detailed assessment, EcomWorld found that while some teams did an excellent job, others fell short of expectations. The analysis showed that the less successful teams had problems with clarity of roles and responsibilities and lacked direction.

Based on these results, EcomWorld introduced a clear definition and documentation of roles and responsibilities within each squad and tribe. In addition, training was provided to deepen the understanding of the roles. In the months that followed, the productivity of these teams increased and they were able to achieve the goals they had set.

Both case studies demonstrate the importance of review and adaptation when implementing the Spotify model. The ability to make changes based on the results is critical to the success of the model. It's not about implementing the model perfectly, but adapting it to your organization's unique needs and challenges.

4.4 Strategy adjustments based on performance

Transitioning to a new operating model like the Spotify model is not a static process. It is a dynamic process that requires flexibility and adaptability. Constant assessment of performance and continuous strategy adjustment are integral to this transition. In this section, we look at how companies can make strategy adjustments based on performance.

Feedback value

Feedback is a powerful source of information that can help understand current performance and shape future performance. It can be done at different levels: individually, as a team (squad), at the tribe level, or even organization-wide. Feedback can come from formal assessments, peer reviews, customer feedback, and many other sources.

Feedback helps identify both strengths and areas for improvement. It enables teams to focus on specific aspects of their work, improve their performance, and thus better align strategy with their goals. It is therefore important to create mechanisms for regular feedback and to foster a culture of openness and constructive dialogue.

Adaptation of processes

Processes also need to be reviewed and adjusted. It may be that certain processes were effective in the early stages of implementing the Spotify model, but have lost their effectiveness over time. Perhaps circumstances have changed or there are better methods to achieve the goals. In such cases, consideration should be given to adjusting the processes.

Change of roles and responsibilities

Roles and responsibilities in Squads and Tribes can also change based on performance. Sometimes a member's skills or strengths may be better utilized in a different role. Or perhaps a person is having difficulty with his or her current role and would be more effective in a different position. It is important to recognize such cases and make adjustments as necessary.

Realignment of goals

Goals should not be static. They should be reviewed regularly and realigned as needed. If a goal is not being met, why that is should be investigated. Is it because of the strategies and tactics used to achieve it? Or is the goal itself no longer relevant or too ambitious? These questions can help make the right adjustments.

Conclusion

Overall, strategy alignment based on performance requires constant assessment and monitoring of performance at various levels. It requires the ability to give and accept feedback, review and adjust processes, change roles and responsibilities, and realign goals. By aligning strategy with performance, an organization can get the most out of the Spotify model and achieve its goals more effectively.

Adjustment of the implementation strategy based on performance data

Moving to the Spotify model is a complex process that requires authoritative strategic decisions. Like any other strategic initiative, the implementation of this model should be based on solid data. Performance data provides an objective basis for evaluating the current situation and enables informed decisions about future steps.

SPOTIFY MODEL: PRACTICAL IMPLEMENTATION GUIDE

Data collection

Performance data can cover a variety of aspects, including productivity, efficiency, quality of work, team dynamics, and employee satisfaction. Some of these data can be measured quantitatively, such as the number of tasks completed or the time to complete a project. Others are more qualitative, such as feedback from employees or customers.

It is important that data collection is systematic and consistent to provide a reliable basis for analysis and decision-making. Tools such as performance dashboards, analysis platforms and feedback tools can help.

Data analysis and interpretation

After data collection, the next step is analysis. Here, it is important to look at the data in context and try to identify patterns and correlations. For example, high productivity rates could indicate efficient work, but if they are accompanied by low employee satisfaction, it could be a sign of excessive stress.

Interpreting the data requires an understanding of both the data itself and the context in which it was generated. It is important to consider both the strengths and weaknesses that the data reveal.

Strategy adjustment

Based on the findings from the data analysis, adjustments can be made to the implementation strategy. For example, if the data indicates that certain teams are having difficulty transitioning to the Spotify model, additional training or resources may be needed.

At the same time, the data could reveal areas in which the company is particularly successful. These strengths can serve as a basis for the further development of the strategy.

Continuous monitoring

Adjusting strategy based on performance data is not a one-time process. Rather, it is an ongoing cycle of data collection, analysis, adjustment, and monitoring. Through continuous monitoring, companies can identify trends, track changes over time, and adjust their strategies accordingly.

Applying performance data to implement the Spotify model enables organizations to make informed, data-driven decisions. It helps them refine their strategies and continuously improve to achieve their goals and drive real change.

Involving employees in the process of strategy adaptation

One of the cornerstones of the Spotify model is the self-organization and autonomy of the teams. This principle can and should also be applied to the strategy alignment process. By actively involving employees in this process, companies can increase employee engagement and satisfaction, gain valuable insights, and make better decisions.

Communication and transparency

The first step in involving employees in the strategy adaptation process is open and transparent communication. Employees should be informed about the company's current performance, the insights gained and the resulting strategic considerations.

This creates a climate of trust and openness in which employees feel safe to express their opinions and ideas. Tools such as intranets, regular updates or town hall meetings can help disseminate information and stimulate discussion.

Feedback and consultation

Employees are often a source of invaluable insight, as they best understand the day-to-day challenges and opportunities of the job. By soliciting their feedback and taking their opinions into account, companies can effectively adapt and improve their strategies.

Feedback can be solicited in a variety of ways, including surveys, one-on-one interviews, focus groups, or brainstorming sessions. Regardless of the method chosen, it is important that employees feel that their feedback is taken seriously and that they have an influence on decision-making processes.

Participative decision making

Another way to involve employees in the strategy adaptation process is through participative decision-making. This means that employees are directly involved in the formulation and selection of strategic options.

This can be done through workshops, planning sessions, or other collaborative formats. It may also mean that teams have some autonomy to make their own decisions and adapt their ways of working, based on their own experience and insights.

Involving employees in the strategy alignment process is an effective way to increase employee engagement, make better decisions, and facilitate strategy implementation. By actively involving the people who put the strategy into practice, companies can ensure that their strategies are based on reality and take into account the needs and capabilities of their employees.

Case studies and examples of strategy adaptations in organizations that have implemented the Spotify model

In the following sections, we will present several case studies and real-world examples to give a sense of what strategy adaptations can look like in organizations that have implemented the Spotify model.

Case study 1: A software development company

Our first example concerns a medium-sized software development company that decided to implement the Spotify model. However, after the first six months of implementation, it became apparent that performance in some teams was below expectations. In particular, the monitoring data showed problems with inter-team collaboration and communication.

Company leaders responded by conducting a comprehensive implementation review and making strategy adjustments. They introduced "Guilds" (professional communities) to promote knowledge sharing and improve communication between teams. They also introduced regular feedback sessions to enable ongoing review and adjustment of implementation.

Case study 2: An e-commerce company

The second example is a large e-commerce company that implemented the Spotify model to scale its operational capabilities. However, after some time it turned out that the changes made did not lead to the expected productivity increases.

After a thorough analysis, the company found that despite implementing the Spotify model, it was stuck with rigid, bureaucratic processes that were limiting efficiency. In response, the company adjusted its strategy and began simplifying its processes and devolving more autonomy to individual squads.

Case study 3: A financial services company

Our final example is a financial services company that implemented the Spotify model to increase its innovation capability. Despite some successes, however, it became apparent that the speed of innovation was still falling short of the company's goals.

Company executives responded by adjusting their strategy and introducing "innovation labs" - dedicated teams focused on exploring new technologies and business opportunities. In addition, incentive systems were revised to encourage more innovation.

In all three cases, the companies were able to adjust their strategies based on performance and data collected. This demonstrates the importance of monitoring, evaluation, and adaptation in the implementation of the Spotify model.

4.5 Iterative improvements

Iterative improvements are at the heart of the agile methodology and a central aspect of the Spotify model. Through repeated adjustments, experiments, and improvements, the iterative approach enables a learning and evolving organizational system that is continuously optimized. In the context of implementing the Spotify model, this means that each phase, process, and outcome is constantly scrutinized and improved.

What does iteration mean?

An iteration is a complete development cycle consisting of several phases: planning, implementation, testing, and reflection. In the context of the Spotify model, the iterative approach enables teams to continuously adapt and improve their ways of working to achieve better results.

The importance of experiments

Iterative improvement requires a culture that encourages and celebrates experimentation. In a culture that encourages experimentation, mistakes are not viewed as failures, but as learning opportunities. If a particular method or process is not producing the desired results, the team should be encouraged to try alternative approaches.

Experiments can take many different forms. It may be the testing of a new working method, the application of a new technology, or the implementation of a new communication structure. Regardless of the context, the goal of any experiment should be to gain valuable insights and drive continuous improvement.

Reflection and adaptation

At the end of each iteration is the reflection. This is a structured review of what worked well and what could be improved. This may involve the team collecting feedback, discussing lessons learned, and developing improvement plans.

These reflections lead to adjustments - changes in the team's way of working, processes or strategy. These adjustments are then carried over into the next iteration, continuing the cycle of continuous improvement.

The role of management

Management plays a critical role in fostering iterative improvement. Managers must create an environment where experimentation and reflection are encouraged and celebrated. They should also serve as role models by constantly questioning and improving their own work and strategy.

In summary

Iterative improvement is a powerful tool for implementing the Spotify model. Through repeated experimentation, reflection, and adaptation, organizations can create a learning and evolving system that is continuously optimized and improved. In an ever-changing world, such agile and adaptive organizations can better respond to challenges, capitalize on opportunities, and achieve sustainable success.

Introduction to the concept of iterative improvement in the context of the Spotify model.

At the heart of implementing the Spotify model is iterative improvement, a method based on repeated cycles of planning, implementation, review, and adjustment. The idea is simple: you put a plan into action, evaluate the results, and make adjustments based on the findings. Then you repeat this cycle - creating a continuous learning and improvement process. In the context of the Spotify model, this principle plays an important role as it helps to continuously optimize team performance and refine the implementation of the model.

The Spotify model envisions that teams' work processes are organized in cycles or "iterations." Each iteration involves a series of activities ranging from planning a product feature or improvement, to executing the work, to reviewing and reflecting on the work done.

The strength of this approach lies in its ability to continuously improve both the product and the process. By focusing on small, incremental changes rather than large, revolutionary changes, teams can respond more flexibly to challenges, minimize risks, and improve the quality of their work.

But to take full advantage of iterative improvement, the principle must be applied not only to products or projects, but also to work processes and structures. For example, the way meetings are held or decisions are made can be regularly reviewed and improved.

It is equally important to foster a culture of continuous improvement where feedback and reflection are valued and mistakes are seen as learning opportunities rather than failures. In the Spotify model, this culture is a central aspect and forms the basis for the effective use of iterative improvement processes.

Overall, iterative improvement provides a powerful method for optimizing team performance and increasing the effectiveness of the Spotify model. Through continuous learning and adaptation, organizations can constantly evolve and improve to succeed in today's rapidly changing business environment.

How to collect and use feedback to make iterative improvements

Feedback is a critical element in implementing the Spotify model and plays a central role in driving iterative improvements. It can come from a variety of sources, including team members, managers, customers, and stakeholders. Here are some strategies for collecting and using feedback to make iterative improvements.

Feedback collection

First and foremost, it is important to establish a systematic process for collecting feedback. This could include regular team meetings, one-on-one conversations or surveys. For example, you could hold weekly or monthly "retrospectives" where team members talk openly about their experiences, challenges and ideas.

Technology tools can also be helpful. There are many feedback and survey tools that teams can use to gain valuable insights. However, the most important thing is to create an open and trusting atmosphere where people feel comfortable giving honest and constructive feedback.

Analysis and implementation of the feedback

Once the feedback is collected, it is important to carefully analyze and prioritize it. You should try to identify patterns and recurring themes that might indicate deeper problems. The findings should then be translated into concrete actions.

A key aspect here is the involvement of the team in the improvement process. Instead of imposing changes from above, team members should have the opportunity to collaborate on the solutions. This promotes commitment and ownership and contributes to more effective implementation of the improvements.

Feedback loops

Feedback should not be a one-time event, but a continuous process. This is the concept of feedback loops. After changes have been implemented, feedback should be collected again to assess whether the changes were successful and whether further adjustments are needed. This continuous loop of feedback and improvement allows an organization to continually adapt and improve.

In summary, feedback is a powerful tool for iterative improvement in the context of the Spotify model. Through effective collection, analysis, and implementation of feedback, an organization can continuously learn, adapt, and grow.

Case studies and examples of iterative improvements in organizations that have implemented the Spotify model.

One of the most compelling examples of iterative improvement in organizations that have implemented the Spotify model comes from the technology industry.

Case Study 1: Tech Company Alpha

Tech Company Alpha is a global technology leader that decided to implement the Spotify model to increase agility and innovation. Initially, the model was implemented strictly according to the predefined principles, but it quickly became apparent that some aspects did not fit well with the company culture.

Through a robust feedback loop that included both formal and informal channels, the company was able to quickly identify where adjustments were needed. For example, the company found that while the concept of autonomous squads led to increased productivity, it also led to some isolation between teams. To address this, they introduced "community of practice" meetings to foster collaboration and knowledge sharing across squad boundaries.

Case study 2: Beta financial services provider

Another example is financial services provider Beta, an established company in a traditionally conservative industry. In moving to the Spotify model, they encountered a number of challenges, particularly around management and employee buy-in. However, through iterative improvements and a culture of constant adaptation, they managed to overcome these obstacles.

An important step was to hold regular retrospectives where teams discussed their experiences and made suggestions for improvement. In addition, the company relied more on training and coaching to ensure that all employees understood and accepted the new ways of working.

These case studies show that implementing the Spotify model is an ongoing process that requires iterative improvements and adjustments. By using effective feedback mechanisms and a culture of continuous improvement, organizations can successfully adapt the model to their specific needs.

Part 5: Further development of the Spotify model

While the Spotify model originated in a single company, it has since evolved into a concept used in many organizations around the world. However, like any model or framework, the Spotify model is subject to constant change and must evolve to remain relevant and effective. In this part, we explore how the Spotify model can evolve to meet the ever-changing needs of the business world.

Above all, we need to remember that the Spotify model is not a rigid set of rules, but a dynamic framework that leaves room for adjustments and modifications. It was not developed as a rigid, unchanging system, but as a flexible model that allows companies to go their own way while benefiting from the principles of agile.

The most important thing we can learn from Spotify's success story is that there is no "one size fits all" business. Every company has its own specific challenges, goals, and contexts that need to be considered.

Therefore, it is critical to look at the Spotify model as a starting point and then adapt and expand it to fit each company's specific needs and circumstances.

With this understanding in mind, in this part we look at the various aspects involved in the evolution of the Spotify model. In doing so, we will focus on both theoretical approaches and practical use cases to develop a comprehensive understanding of what the Spotify model could look like in the future.

As we look at the future evolution of the Spotify model, we will also discuss some of the challenges that may come with these changes and identify ways to overcome them. Through this combination of theory and practice, we will gain a clear and comprehensive insight into the potential future of the Spotify model.

In this section, expect in-depth discussions and case studies that highlight the dynamic and flexible nature of the Spotify model. It's not just about what the model is, but what it could be. This allows us to explore the boundaries of what is possible with the Spotify model and understand how we can use this powerful tool to continue to make our organizations successful in an ever-changing business world.

5.1 Further improvements in cooperation

Collaboration is the backbone of any successful organization and a core principle of the Spotify model. In this section, we look at additional collaboration enhancement opportunities that can not only strengthen teamwork, but also improve overall organizational performance. These enhancements build on the solid foundation provided by the Spotify model and introduce new concepts and practices to make collaboration even more effective.

A key aspect we will address in this chapter is improving communication. Communication is a critical component in collaboration and can make the difference between the success and failure of a project. We will explore how implementing new communication techniques and tools can improve communication within squads, tribes, chapters, and guilds.

Another important area we will look at is collaboration across teams and departments. The Spotify model places a high value on collaboration within squads, but how can we ensure that this high level of collaboration is maintained across squads? Here we look at strategies and best practices for fostering interdisciplinary collaboration and overcoming silo thinking.

We will also look at the concept of "Deep Work" and how it can improve collaboration and productivity. "Deep Work" is a term introduced by author and professor Cal Newport to describe the state of intense focus and concentration required for complex tasks. We will discuss how the principles of "Deep Work" can be integrated into the work culture of a Spotify team and the impact this can have on collaboration.

We will also look at how technologies such as artificial intelligence and machine learning can improve collaboration. These technologies offer a wealth of opportunities to improve communication, coordination and decision-making in teams and can help take collaboration to the next level.

By combining these different approaches and techniques, we provide a comprehensive overview of the opportunities for advancing collaboration in organizations that have implemented the Spotify model. Our goal is to provide a pathway for how these enhancements can improve performance and productivity while fostering a positive and supportive work culture.

Techniques and strategies to further improve collaboration within the Spotify model.

One of the greatest strengths of the Spotify model is its emphasis on collaboration and teamwork. However, there is always room for improvement and growth. In this section, we will explore a number of techniques and strategies that can further improve collaboration within the Spotify model.

Let's start with communication, a key element of collaboration. Effective communication is critical to ensuring that all members of a squad or tribe are on the same page and share a common vision. Therefore, organizations should continually introduce new communication techniques and tools that improve information transfer and reduce misunderstandings. For example, digital communication platforms that enable real-time collaboration and shared document management can greatly facilitate collaboration across distributed teams.

Another aspect of collaboration that can be improved is the interaction between different squads and tribes. Often silos can develop when teams work independently of each other, which can lead to fragmentation of efforts. To overcome this, organizations can implement methods to encourage interdisciplinary collaboration, such as regular inter-tribal meetings where teams can present their work and receive feedback from others.

Next, we could take a closer look at the concept of "Deep Work." This method, coined by Cal Newport, emphasizes the importance of undisturbed concentration in complex tasks and could significantly increase productivity and creativity in squads and tribes. Part of this method could be to integrate "Deep Work" blocks into the work schedule, where employees can work on their projects undisturbed.

Finally, we could use advanced technologies such as artificial intelligence and machine learning to improve collaboration. These technologies can help streamline work processes, improve communication, and facilitate decision-making processes. For example, machine learning models could be used to analyze work habits and provide personalized recommendations to improve productivity and collaboration.

In summary, there are many opportunities to further enhance collaboration within the Spotify model. By implementing new communication techniques, fostering interdisciplinary collaboration, incorporating "deep work" principles, and leveraging advanced technologies, organizations can maximize the benefits of this model and create an even stronger, more effective, and more creative work environment.

How to use feedback and evaluation systems to improve collaboration

The importance of feedback and assessments in a work environment cannot be overstated, especially in the Spotify model of self-organization, learning, and continuous improvement. They allow us to monitor performance, improve the quality of work, and foster professional growth. So how can we effectively use feedback and evaluation systems to improve collaboration?

First, it is important to foster an open feedback culture. Fear of criticism can often lead to a negative feedback loop where employees are reluctant to give or receive honest feedback. By creating an environment where constructive feedback is valued and encouraged, an organization can improve the flow of information and create an atmosphere of continuous improvement.

In addition, it is helpful to establish a formal process for collecting and analyzing feedback. This could be achieved through regular performance appraisals or 360-degree feedback mechanisms, where employees receive feedback from their peers, supervisors and subordinates. Such systems can help uncover hidden problems, improve collaboration and enhance team performance.

Evaluation systems can also help improve collaboration by clarifying expectations and setting goals. They can be used to track progress against goals and recognize individual contributions to team performance. However, it is important that such systems are fair, transparent and based on clear criteria to encourage employee engagement and motivation.

Another important aspect of using feedback and evaluation systems is a willingness to adapt. It is unlikely that a system, once set up, will be perfect. Therefore, it is important to regularly collect feedback and refine the system based on this feedback. Feedback should be collected not only from employees, but also from customers and other stakeholders to ensure a comprehensive perspective.

Finally, feedback should always be future-oriented. Instead of focusing on past mistakes, the focus should be on what can be improved in the future. This promotes a positive atmosphere and encourages employees to learn from their mistakes and develop further.

Overall, feedback and evaluation systems can be a powerful tool for improving collaboration within the Spotify model. By fostering an open feedback culture, establishing formal processes, clarifying expectations and goals, being willing to adapt, and taking a forward-looking approach, organizations can improve collaboration and foster a culture of continuous improvement.

Case studies and examples of successful collaboration improvements

One of the organizations that have successfully implemented the Spotify model is global software company ABC. ABC has undergone an organizational transformation to become more agile and improve the way it works. It has adapted the organizational structure of the Spotify model and implemented feedback and evaluation systems to improve collaboration.

As part of this initiative, ABC fostered a culture of continuous learning and improvement. It implemented a system of "chapter leads" who acted as coaches for smaller, subject-specific teams and provided regular, constructive feedback. It also implemented an evaluation system that assessed team performance and the contribution of individual members, based on clearly defined criteria. These criteria were focused on the achievement of business objectives and also took into account soft factors such as teamwork and commitment.

Another outstanding example is the US company TRTs. It is known for its unique corporate culture and the high value it places on employee satisfaction. TRTs has integrated the Spotify model into its structure and successfully implemented a number of techniques and strategies to improve collaboration.

One of the most notable features at TRTs is the peer review system. Employees are encouraged to evaluate their peers, which leads to a culture of recognition and appreciation. In addition, TRTs has introduced the concept of "link bubbles," where small teams or "bubbles" are formed based on specific projects or initiatives. This encourages collaboration by allowing employees to use their skills and interests to contribute beyond their regular role.

These case studies illustrate how implementing feedback and evaluation systems and adapting specific techniques and strategies from the Spotify model can help improve collaboration in different organizational environments. While each organization is unique and requires a customized approach, these examples provide valuable insights on how to optimize the process of collaboration and foster a culture of continuous improvement and learning.

5.2 Promoting agility in the organization

In today's dynamic business environment, it is critical to be agile - that is, to have the ability to adapt quickly to changing circumstances, whether they are new technologies, market conditions, or customer expectations. An organization that promotes agility can respond more effectively to change, overcoming both internal and external challenges. The Spotify model can be an effective way to foster this agility.

Let's start by explaining the concept of "agility". Agility in an organizational context refers to a company's ability to adapt quickly to change, respond flexibly to new challenges, and remain both efficient and effective. This ability is particularly invaluable at a time when technological change and market volatility have become commonplace.

To promote agility in an organization, a culture of openness and adaptability must first be created. This means that both managers and employees must be willing to embrace new ideas, see mistakes as learning opportunities, and view change as an opportunity rather than a threat. In the Spotify model, this is achieved by promoting "autonomy." Teams working as autonomous units are able to respond more quickly and flexibly to change because they do not have to wait for approval or instructions from above.

Another key to driving agility is communication. Effective communication ensures that information flows quickly and accurately throughout the organization, which in turn enables faster decision making and problem solving. In the Spotify model, this is achieved by establishing "Guilds," interdisciplinary groups that meet regularly to share knowledge and work together on challenges.

However, to truly promote agility in the organization requires more than just structural changes. It requires a shift in thinking and behavior at the individual and collective level. It requires employees to be willing to take risks, to take initiative, and to constantly strive to improve both themselves and the organization.

Promoting agility can be a challenging task, but the rewards are worth it. Agile organizations are more resilient, innovative, and responsive to their customers' needs. By implementing the Spotify model and fostering a culture of openness, adaptability and continuous improvement, any organization can reap the benefits of agility.

Methods for promoting agility in teams and the entire organization

To promote agility in a company, a number of specific measures and methods are required. These methods take into account both organizational structure and culture and require the commitment of everyone involved, from managers to employees. Here are some best practices for promoting agility.

- Promoting autonomy: Autonomy is a key concept in the Spotify model and plays an important role in promoting agility. Autonomous teams have the freedom to make decisions and solve problems without constant interference or control from above. This can reduce response time and allow teams to be more creative and innovative.

● Training and education: Agility requires specific skills and knowledge, such as managing uncertainty, learning and adapting quickly, and understanding agile principles and methods. Training and education programs can help employees acquire and strengthen these skills.

● Encourage communication and collaboration: Fostering open and effective communication within and between teams is critical to agility. This can be achieved by setting up regular meetings, using collaboration tools, and encouraging open and transparent information sharing.

● Implement iterative processes: Agile organizations work iteratively and incrementally, which means they work in small steps and regularly integrate feedback and learning into their processes. This can be achieved through agile methods such as Scrum or Kanban.

● Develop a culture of error: To foster agility, organizations must create a culture where mistakes are viewed as learning opportunities. This encourages employees to take risks and try out new ideas, which in turn promotes innovation and adaptability.

● Leaders as role models: Leaders play a critical role in promoting agility. They should act as role models by exemplifying agile values and practices, promoting openness and transparency, and encouraging employees to self-organize and continuously improve.

Adopting these methods can help create an agile culture and maximize the benefits of agility. However, it is important to emphasize that agile is not a one-time project, but requires an ongoing effort and involves constant adjustments and improvements. Implementing the Spotify model can be an effective way to initiate and lead this change.

Application of agile principles to organizational structure and processes

Agile principles were originally developed for software development, but they are just as relevant and valuable when applied to organizational structure and processes. It is about creating a culture based on collaboration, flexibility, learning and adaptation.

Structural adjustments

Decentralized decision making: At the heart of agile principles is the idea of decentralized decision making. This means that decisions are made as close as possible to where the work actually gets done. In practical terms, this means minimizing hierarchies and giving teams the autonomy to make their own decisions.

Cross-functional teams: Agile organizations rely on cross-functional teams, i.e. teams consisting of members with different expertise and skills. This type of structure promotes collaboration and enables teams to work faster and more efficiently because they have all the necessary resources within the team.

Adaptations of the processes

Iterative processes: Agile principles emphasize the importance of iteration and continuous learning. Rather than planning and implementing large projects in one piece, agile organizations work in short cycles that allow them to regularly gather feedback and make adjustments.

Introducing Scrum or Kanban: Scrum and Kanban are agile methods that can help structure and organize work processes. Scrum is ideal for projects that have complex tasks and high unpredictability, while Kanban is well suited for continuous workflows.

Promote a culture of error: Agile organizations view mistakes not as failures, but as learning opportunities. They enact mechanisms that encourage teams to take risks and test new ideas, and they provide them with the support and resources they need to learn from mistakes and improve.

Continuous improvement: A central aspect of agile is the idea of continuous improvement. Agile organizations enact processes and practices that encourage teams to constantly look for ways to improve their work, and they give them the autonomy and resources they need to implement those improvements.

Implementing agile principles is not always easy and often requires significant changes in organizational structure and culture. But the benefits, such as increased flexibility, faster response times, and an improved ability to react to change, can more than make up for the challenges. Implementing the Spotify model can be a helpful tool to support this process.

Case studies and examples of successfully improved agility

Case study 1: ABC

ABC, a Dutch multinational bank, implemented a comprehensive agile transformation to support their digitization efforts. They restructured their entire organization using the Spotify model, organizing thousands of employees into small "squads" that work autonomously.

By adopting this model, ABC has been able to bring its products to market faster and improve customer satisfaction. With the help of cross-functional teams working autonomously and in close collaboration, ABC has also been able to significantly reduce the time needed for product development. This new working model has enabled ABC to respond agilely and quickly to changing market requirements.

Case study 2: BY

BY Group, a leading global technology and services company, introduced agile methods to reduce product development time and achieve greater customer focus. They relied on Scrum and Kanban to structure and control their development processes.

By implementing these agile methods, BY was able to significantly reduce product development times. It also enabled them to align their products more closely with their customers' needs by putting the customer at the center of their development processes and collecting regular feedback.

Case study 3: General Electric

General Electric (GE) is another company that has successfully implemented agile principles. At GE, they introduced a method known as "FastWorks" based on the principles of Lean Startup.

With FastWorks, GE focused on developing minimum viable products (MVPs) and bringing them to market quickly to gather feedback and iterate. This enabled GE to respond more quickly to market changes and develop innovative products that are closely aligned with customer needs.

These case studies show how companies of different sizes and from different industries have been able to improve their agility by implementing agile principles and methods. Each company had to find its own way to implement and adapt these principles and methods to fit their specific needs and challenges. But regardless of the specific methods they implemented, all of these companies were able to reap the benefits of increased agility: faster response times, increased customer satisfaction, and improved ability to deliver innovative products and services.

5.3 Optimization of customer orientation

Customer focus is at the heart of every successful organization. Customers are the lifeblood of any business, and their feedback is invaluable for improving products and services, generating new ideas, and better understanding the market. The Spotify model provides a unique platform to optimize customer centricity through its agile structure and culture based on autonomy, collaboration, and continuous learning. In this section, we will focus on how companies can leverage the Spotify model to optimize customer centricity.

The first step in improving customer focus is to understand customer needs. This can be achieved by gathering direct feedback from customers, conducting customer surveys, and making efforts to understand customers and their behavior. In autonomous teams, such as those in the Spotify model, each member has direct contact with customers, deepening the understanding of customer needs throughout the organization.

Another crucial aspect is the integration of customer feedback into the development process. In the Spotify model, this is done through regular retrospectives and reviews where customer feedback is discussed and plans for improvement are created. Through constant iteration and improvement, companies can respond quickly to feedback and make changes tailored to customer needs.

Optimizing customer orientation also requires a culture of learning and adaptation. In the Spotify model, this is achieved by encouraging experimentation and failure as a learning opportunity. By trying out new ideas and learning from mistakes, teams can develop innovative solutions that meet customer needs.

In addition, "Guilds" and "Chapters" in the Spotify model play a crucial role in promoting customer orientation. They provide platforms for sharing best practices, ideas, and experiences aimed at improving customer orientation.

Optimizing customer centricity is not a one-time process, but an ongoing effort that requires continuous monitoring of customer needs, regular feedback, and constant adjustments. With its agile structure and culture, the Spotify model provides a solid foundation for optimizing customer centricity and helps companies better understand and serve their customers.

Strategies for improving customer focus using the Spotify model.

Improving customer orientation is a key strategic priority for companies that want to succeed in today's competitive business environment. Within the Spotify model, there are several strategies that can be used to optimize customer orientation.

Incorporating customer feedback into the product development cycle: The Spotify model emphasizes the importance of working closely with customers and integrating their feedback into the product development cycle. By using methodologies such as Lean UX and agile, teams can work closely with customers, understand their needs, and respond quickly to their feedback.

Building a learning culture: Another important aspect is building a learning culture where experimentation and mistakes are seen as opportunities to learn and grow. This culture promotes continuous improvement and innovation, which ultimately leads to better products and services for customers.

Use of data analytics: The use of data analytics can help to better understand customer behavior and preferences. By analyzing customer interactions, purchase behavior, and other data, valuable insights can be gained that can be used to improve the customer experience.

Establish cross-functional teams: In the Spotify model, teams are cross-functional and autonomous, meaning they have the ability to respond quickly to customer feedback and make changes. These teams are also responsible for understanding customer needs and developing solutions to meet those needs.

Fostering collaboration and knowledge sharing: The Spotify model's structure of Tribes, Squads, Chapters, and Guilds fosters collaboration and knowledge sharing. This enables teams to learn from the experiences and best practices of others and optimize their strategies to improve customer centricity.

In summary, improving customer orientation is a strategic priority that requires continuous attention and effort. By applying the above strategies, companies can effectively use the Spotify model to optimize their customer orientation.

Integration of customer feedback and adaptation of processes to improve customer orientation

Integrating customer feedback into work processes is a key strategy for improving customer focus within the Spotify model. It enables a direct link between users and product development teams, ensuring that products and services actually meet customers' needs and expectations.

First, it is important to establish effective channels for collecting customer feedback. This can be achieved through various methods, including surveys, interviews, user forums, social media interactions, and analysis of customer data. These feedback channels should be clearly communicated and easily accessible to customers.

After collecting the feedback comes the crucial phase of analyzing and integrating this feedback into the product development cycle. This is where agility and flexibility are essential. Agile methods enable teams to respond quickly to feedback by making adjustments to products or services or implementing new features.

An important aspect of this is iterative design, which is characterized by the philosophy of "Fail Fast, Learn Fast". Instead of waiting for a complete and perfect solution, products or services are provided in a basic version, the so-called Minimal Viable Product (MVP). Customer usage and feedback on the MVP then lead to rapid iterations and improvements to the offering.

Another key to improving customer focus is a willingness to change processes based on customer feedback. This may mean revising existing workflows, discarding inefficient practices and introducing new methods. In a learning organization, this ability to adapt and change is critical.

Integrating customer feedback and adapting processes are thus effective strategies for improving customer orientation within the Spotify model. By maintaining a constant dialog with customers and responding quickly to their needs and wishes, companies can achieve stronger customer loyalty and greater business success.

Case studies and examples of successfully improved customer orientation

The implementation of customer orientation in an organization can vary depending on the industry, product or service. The following case studies and examples show how different companies have used the Spotify model to improve their customer orientation.

Case study 1: A technology platform

A technology company that offers a software-as-a-service (SaaS) platform implemented the Spotify model to improve its customer experience. Previously, the company had received feedback from customers that the platform was too complex and difficult to navigate.

The company organized its product development teams into squads, each focused on specific features of the platform. Each of these squads integrated customer feedback directly into their work processes. They used agile methods to respond to customer feedback and make changes to the platform. This approach enabled the company to build a closer relationship with its customers and improve its platform based on their needs.

Case study 2: A retail company

A retail company with physical stores and an online sales channel was looking for ways to improve customer focus. Using the Spotify model, the company organized its employees into cross-functional teams, each responsible for specific customer segments or product categories.

These teams worked closely with customers, collecting feedback and using it to optimize the product range and customer experience. Through regular retrospective meetings, the teams were able to continuously improve their processes and respond to customer feedback. These changes led to higher customer satisfaction and brand engagement.

Case study 3: A fintech start-up

A fintech startup offering digital payment solutions used the Spotify model to respond quickly to market changes and customer needs. The product development teams worked in squads and used agile methods to organize their work.

By incorporating customer feedback into the product development process, the start-up has been able to continuously improve its digital payment solutions and adapt them to the needs of its customers.

These case studies show how the Spotify model can help improve customer centricity. Although each company is unique, the principles and methods shown in these examples can be applied in a variety of ways to improve customer centricity in any organization.

5.4 Adaptations and modifications of the model

The Spotify model provides an excellent blueprint for a more agile and collaborative organizational structure. But as with any template, it is important to understand that adaptations and modifications may be necessary to tailor the model to the specific needs and contexts of different organizations. This section addresses the customization options and modifications that organizations can make to better fit the Spotify model to their unique circumstances.

Every organization has its unique culture, business goals, and operational reality. Therefore, it may be necessary to adapt the Spotify model in order to implement it effectively within your own organization. Adaptations may be necessary to overcome certain challenges or limitations due to the size of the organization, the nature of the work, the skills and competencies available, the culture of the organization, or other specific factors.

For example, some organizations might modify the concept of "squads" and "tribes" to fit their specific operational conditions. For example, a technology company might decide to organize its squads by technical specialty, while a retail company might organize them by product category or market segment.

In addition, an organization with a highly hierarchical and bureaucratic culture might find that it needs to introduce the Spotify model gradually to ensure a successful transformation. It could start by introducing agile methods to a few select teams before rolling out the model to the entire organization.

Another common adaptation concerns the role of the "Product Owner". In the Spotify model, the product owner is typically responsible for leading a squad and defining the product vision. However, in some organizations, it might make sense to modify or expand this role to include other functions such as marketing, sales, or customer service.

It is also important to note that the Spotify model, while heavily based on agile methods, does not necessarily align with all aspects of agile philosophy or practice. Some organizations might therefore adapt the model to better align with their existing agile practices or values.

Overall, it is critical to view the Spotify model as a flexible template that can be modified and adapted to meet the specific needs and challenges of each organization. Successful implementation requires a deep understanding of one's organizational circumstances and a willingness to continuously learn and adapt. It is an ongoing process of iteration and improvement, driven by a strong commitment to agility, collaboration, and customer focus.

Overview of possible adjustments to the Spotify model to improve performance.

The Spotify model is not a one-size-fits-all approach. Rather, it is a dynamic framework designed to promote agility, collaboration and innovation. This framework can and should be customized to meet the specific needs and goals of each organization to achieve optimal results. Below, we discuss some possible adaptations to the Spotify model to improve performance.

Squad size and composition

In the original Spotify model, a squad consists of 6 to 12 people working on a common product or project. However, depending on the nature of the work and the specific needs of the organization, squads can be smaller or larger. The composition of squads can also be changed to include different skills and expertise.

Structure and role of tribes

The Tribe structure in the Spotify model aims to foster communication and collaboration between Squads. However, in some organizations, it might make sense to adjust the structure and role of Tribes. For example, an organization might organize Tribes by functional area (e.g., marketing, technology, sales) rather than by product or project.

Integration of Guilds and Chapters

The involvement of Guilds and Chapters is a central aspect of the Spotify model. These entities enable knowledge transfer and professional development within the organization. However, depending on the specific needs of the organization, additional Guilds or Chapters might be required, or their role might be changed to address specific goals or challenges.

Adaptation of agile practices

Although the Spotify model is heavily based on agile practices, it might be necessary to adapt or modify these practices to better fit the specific needs of the organization. For example, an organization might decide to incorporate certain aspects of Scrum, Kanban, or Lean into its workflows, depending on the specific needs and challenges of its work.

Continuous improvement and adaptation

Perhaps most importantly, the Spotify model is based on the idea of continuous improvement and adaptation. This means that organizations should regularly review the effectiveness of their model and make necessary changes to improve their performance. This could be done through regular reviews, retrospective meetings, employee feedback, and other forms of assessment and reflection.

Ultimately, the most effective adaptations of the Spotify model are those based on a deep understanding of one's organizational culture, structure, and goals. Through continuous learning, experimentation, and adaptation, organizations can leverage the model to foster a stronger culture of agility, collaboration, and customer centricity.

How to make changes based on the specific needs and challenges of the business

Adapting the Spotify model to a company's specific needs and challenges is a delicate task that requires thoughtful strategy and execution. Here are some steps to consider to ensure a seamless transition.

1. understand your organization

The first step to customizing the Spotify model is to have a comprehensive understanding of your organization. This includes knowing your business goals, culture, processes, and dynamics within your teams. Through interviews, surveys, and observations, you can gain a clear picture of your organization's strengths, weaknesses, and opportunities.

2. identify specific needs and challenges

Once you have a clear picture of your organization, identify the specific needs and challenges that the Spotify model could solve. For example, some teams may struggle with communication and coordination, while others may need support with prioritization and work efficiency.

3. design customizations to the Spotify model

Based on your findings, you can begin to design adjustments to the Spotify model. This could include changing the size or composition of squads, adjusting the structure or role of tribes, including additional guilds or chapters, or modifying agile practices. You should also consider how to integrate the Spotify model with existing processes and practices in your organization.

4. implement the adjustments step by step

Once you have designed your customizations, you should implement them in stages. This will give your organization time to get used to the changes and allow you to gather feedback and make adjustments as needed. It may be helpful to start with a pilot project to test the effectiveness of your customizations before rolling them out to the entire organization.

5. continuously check and adjust

Finally, it is important to continuously review the effectiveness of your adjustments and make adjustments as needed. You can use retrospective meetings, surveys, feedback sessions, and other forms of evaluation to do this. Remember that the goal of the Spotify model is continuous improvement, and you should take this approach when adapting the model to your organization.

By following these steps, you can effectively adapt the Spotify model to your organization's specific needs and challenges and help your organization become more agile, collaborative, and customer-centric.

Case studies and examples of successful modifications to the Spotify model.

Over the years, many companies have adapted the Spotify model to meet their specific needs and challenges. In the following, we will look at two such case studies that provide examples of successful modifications to the Spotify model.

Case Study 1: TechStartup Inc.

TechStartup Inc, a growing technology company, faced the challenge of scaling quickly while maintaining a high level of agility and innovation. The company chose the Spotify model, but found that it needed to make some adjustments to adapt it to its specific needs.

One of the changes TechStartup Inc. made was to change the size and composition of its squads. Instead of following the recommended size of eight members, TechStartup Inc. experimented with larger squads of up to 15 members. These squads were interdisciplinary and consisted of members from different areas of expertise to ensure a broader range of skills and perspectives.

In addition, TechStartup Inc. introduced a new element to the model called "focus groups." These were similar to Guilds, but had a more specific role. They focused on specific technology challenges or business goals and worked closely with Squads to find solutions.

The results of these adjustments were impressive. TechStartup Inc. was able to increase its productivity and innovation rate while improving employee satisfaction and engagement.

Case Study 2: FinServ Ltd.

FinServ Ltd, a financial services company, implemented the Spotify model to improve agility and decentralize decision making. However, the company found that it needed to make some modifications to adapt the model to its regulatory requirements and complex organizational structure.

One of the major changes that FinServ Ltd. made was the introduction of an additional layer between the Squads and the Tribes. This was referred to as an "Area" and included several Tribes that operated in similar business areas. This change allowed FinServ Ltd. to ensure effective communication and coordination between the various Tribes while meeting compliance requirements.

In addition to these changes, FinServ Ltd. also modified the roles of Product Owner and Scrum Master to meet regulatory requirements. This included a stronger emphasis on risk management capabilities and closer alignment with the Compliance and Legal teams.

The adjustments FinServ Ltd. has made have helped adapt the Spotify model to the specific needs and challenges of a regulated financial services company. They have led to improved business processes, more efficient decision-making, and higher employee satisfaction.

These two case studies demonstrate that the Spotify model is not intended to be one-size-fits-all for all organizations. Rather, it can and should be adapted to meet the specific needs and challenges of each organization. Through careful consideration and continuous iteration, organizations can successfully modify the model to achieve greater agility, collaboration, and customer centricity.

5.5 Looking to the future: further developments and trends

The horizon of agility and organizational structures is not static, it is constantly evolving and transforming. Companies around the world are continuously learning and adapting to succeed in today's competitive business environment. With the Spotify model firmly in place at many companies, the opportunities for advancements and emerging trends are exciting and far-reaching. Let's take a look at some possible future trends.

1. increased decentralization

One of the core ideas of the Spotify model is decentralization. It allows companies to make decisions closer to those who do the work, often resulting in better quality and faster execution. In the future, this decentralization could deepen by moving more autonomy and decision-making power to the squad level.

In such a model, squads could, for example, have more control over their budgets and resource allocations, allowing them to respond quickly to changes and drive innovation. This would, of course, require a greater emphasis on squad member responsibility and accountability, but the potential benefits could be significant.

2. integration of artificial intelligence and automation

With the advent of artificial intelligence (AI) and automation, we could see these technologies increasingly integrated into squad workflows. For example, AI could be used to predict project outcomes, identify bottlenecks, or improve resource planning.

Automation could help reduce repetitive and time-consuming tasks, giving squads more time to focus on more creative and complex problem solving. In addition, these technologies could help improve communication and collaboration within and between squads, for example by automating certain aspects of reporting and information sharing.

3. expansion of the role of Guilds and Tribes

While the Spotify model already envisions a large role for Guilds and Tribes, we could see an even greater emphasis on these elements in the future. Guilds, for example, could play a greater role in business strategy and planning by contributing their expertise and insights.

At the same time, tribes could increasingly serve as platforms for collaboration and knowledge sharing across squad boundaries. This could be done, for example, through the establishment of "intertribal" projects or initiatives focused on specific strategic goals or challenges.

4. greater emphasis on customer orientation

In the future, we may see an even greater focus on the customer, both in terms of how squads are organized and how they operate. This could mean, for example, that squads are more focused on specific customer segments or needs, or that they build closer relationships with their customers to gain a better understanding of their needs and expectations.

It could also mean that customer feedback and data are used even more in squad decision making and prioritization. This could be supported, for example, by the use of data-driven approaches or customer feedback tools.

In summary, the future of the Spotify model and agility in general is exciting and promising. The trends outlined above are just some of the possibilities, and it is likely that we will see many more innovations and developments in the coming years. Ultimately, the key to success in this ever-changing landscape will be to be open to change, to continuously learn and adapt, and to always focus on delivering value to customers.

Predictions and expectations for the future of the Spotify model

The future of the Spotify model holds a high degree of unpredictability, coupled with great excitement. In the fast-paced world of technological advancement and ever-increasing emphasis on agility, the Spotify model is sure to evolve. But what might that future look like? Here are some predictions and expectations:

1. refinement and improvement of the model

Although the Spotify model has already been implemented in many organizations around the world, there is still plenty of room for refinement and improvement. For example, additional levels of abstraction could be added to the model to enable even better collaboration and coordination between different parts of the organization. Improved methods for feedback and continuous learning could also be introduced to improve performance and drive innovation.

2. adaptation to different corporate cultures and contexts.

The Spotify model originated in a particular corporate culture and context, and it has often been criticized for not transferring well to other environments. However, in the future, it could be modified and adapted to better fit different company cultures and contexts. This could be done by integrating principles and practices from other agile frameworks or management approaches, or by adapting the model to specific industry or market conditions.

3. dissemination in other industries

To date, the Spotify model has been applied primarily in the tech and software development industries. In the future, however, it could become increasingly important in other industries, such as manufacturing, healthcare, or education. In these contexts, the model could help promote agility and flexibility, improve collaboration, and strengthen customer focus.

4. linkage with new technologies

As technology advances, we could see the Spotify model being linked to new technologies, such as Artificial Intelligence, Virtual Reality or Blockchain. These technologies could help improve collaboration and communication in the model, increase transparency, and create new opportunities for innovation and creativity.

It is important to note that these predictions and expectations are based on current trends and observations, and that the actual future of the Spotify model will depend on a variety of factors, including the changing business environment, technological advances, and the specific needs and challenges of the companies implementing the model. It remains exciting to see how the Spotify model will evolve in the coming years.

Trends and innovations in agile organizational development

Several trends and innovations are emerging in agile organizational development that could shape the future. Some of these key trends are:

1. value-based agility

Agile has evolved from a software development tool to a business philosophy. More and more organizations are realizing that agility is more than just a collection of methods and practices - it is a means to create value. This includes a willingness to respond to change and embrace it as an opportunity, rather than viewing it as a risk. Value-based agility focuses on using the principles and practices of agility in a way that maximizes the creation and delivery of value, not just on being agile for agility's sake.

2. AI-driven agility

Artificial intelligence (AI) and machine learning offer great opportunities for agile organizational development. These technologies can help collect and analyze data to make informed decisions, improve performance, and drive innovation. They can also help improve collaboration and communication in agile teams, for example, by enabling automated stand-ups, retrospective analysis, or predictions of team performance.

3. personalized agility

Not every business is the same, and what works for one business doesn't necessarily work for another. Personalized agile means using the principles and practices of agile in a way that fits the specific needs, challenges, and goals of a particular organization. This could involve modifying or adapting the Spotify model or other agile frameworks, or even developing an entirely new framework tailored to the specific context of the business.

4. agility throughout the company

Although agility originated in software development, it is increasingly being applied in other areas of the business, from HR and marketing to finance and operations. This trend is expected to continue to grow as more companies realize that agility can help drive efficiency and innovation across all areas of the business.

5. the focus on the agile culture

In the past, many agile transformations focused on processes and practices. Today, more and more organizations are recognizing that an agile culture - one that promotes flexibility, learning, collaboration and customer centricity - is just as important, if not more so. This trend will likely continue to grow in importance as organizations look for ways to change their culture to support agility.

These trends and innovations show that agile organizational development is a dynamic and constantly changing field. It remains exciting to see how these trends will develop in the coming years and what new innovations will still emerge.

Case studies and examples of innovative applications and advancements of the Spotify model.

To shed light on the continuous change and evolution of the Spotify model, let's take a look at some companies that have innovatively adapted and evolved this model.

1st case study: tech company Alpha Inc.

Alpha Inc, a growing technology company, implemented the Spotify model to improve its team dynamics and accelerate product development. Despite initial success, however, the company encountered challenges related to communication and coordination between different squads and tribes.

Alpha Inc. solved this problem by introducing an "Inter-Squad Coordination Board." This board was used to share all relevant information and updates between different squads while fostering a sense of transparency and collaboration. In addition, an "Inter-Tribe Liaison Officer" was appointed to be responsible for communication between different Tribes. These innovations enabled Alpha Inc. to significantly increase the efficiency of its agile teams and shorten its product development times.

Case study 2: Fintech company Beta Corp.

Beta Corp, a fast-growing fintech company, faced the challenge of managing an increasing number of employees without compromising the speed and quality of its services. Beta Corp. decided to implement the Spotify model, but found that it was struggling to meet the needs and expectations of all employees.

To solve this problem, Beta Corp. decided to create a personalized version of the Spotify model. Each Tribe was asked to create its own model based on its specific needs and challenges. In addition, Tribe leads were encouraged to gather regular feedback and adjust their models accordingly. These innovations helped Beta Corp. increase employee satisfaction, boost productivity and further improve its services.

3rd case study: e-commerce company Gamma Tech

Gamma Tech, a global e-commerce company, used the Spotify model to improve information flow and team collaboration. However, they found that isolating squads led to slower decision making and less innovation.

Gamma Tech solved this problem by introducing "Innovation Labs," where members from different squads and tribes came together to collaborate on new ideas and projects. These labs fostered collaboration, accelerated decision-making, and led to an increased rate of innovation.

These case studies show that there is no "one-size-fits-all" approach to implementing the Spotify model. Organizations can and should adapt the model to their specific needs and challenges to get the most out of their agile approach. This flexibility and adaptability are part of what makes the Spotify model so effective and future-proof.

Milton Keynes UK
Ingram Content Group UK Ltd.
UKHW010626100823
426647UK00001B/58